COPING WITH
ILLNESS

THE·CHRISTIAN·DOCTOR·SERIES

COPING WITH ILLNESS

Dr ROGER HURDING

HODDER AND STOUGHTON
LONDON SYDNEY AUCKLAND TORONTO

Unless stated to the contrary, all Bible references are from the New Internation Version, © 1973, 1978, 1984 by International Bible Society.

British Library Cataloguing in Publication Data

Hurding, Roger F.
   Coping with illness.——(Hodder Christian
paperbacks).
   1. Sick——Prayer-books and devotions——
English
   I. Title
   242'.4   BV4910

  ISBN 0 340 41591 6

Hodder & Stoughton Editorial Office: 47 Bedford Square, London WC1B 3DP.

To Ruth,
niece, friend
and inspiration

CONTENTS

PREFACE

There must be few, if any, people reading these lines who have never been ill, never needed to see a doctor – even as a child with earache or a troublesome cough. Amongst the very high numbers who have had some contact with the medical profession, there will be many who have been 'laid aside' for varying periods of time. For the vast majority this has been through an annual bout of flu, recovery from a minor operation (minor to the surgeon but not to the patient!), resting up after a badly sprained ankle or a slipped disc. For many others, though, there has been more protracted illness, which wears the sufferer down by its recurring nature – like chronic arthritis, intermittent chest infections, longstanding heart disease, kidney trouble, gastric or duodenal ulcers, or multiple sclerosis. Others again have suffered not so much from being ill as from being disabled, perhaps since birth or childhood, or through some devastating injury or stroke later in life. Yet others know the progressive deterioration which can come from serious or fatal illness, as in certain diseases of the nervous system, various forms of cancer, kidney or liver failure, and, perhaps most feared of all, AIDS.

This book is an attempt to help not only those who are 'laid aside', for whatever reason, but also the hidden sufferers, the friends and family members who do their best to care for the ill and disabled. Through telling the stories of people of all ages who face illness or handicap, whether temporary or long-term, chronically debilitating or progressive and fatal, it is hoped that many, both carers and cared for, will find fresh courage to cope with each day.

Behind the stories, and indeed throughout the book, run

the interweaving themes of suffering and healing, loss and gain, the way of the cross and the way of the empty tomb. Everyday life is never one or the other, though most of us, left to our own devices, would opt for healing, gain and the jubilation of Easter morning! These glories, in their full and unblemished state, *are* to be ours in eternity: in the meantime, though we have appetisers of wonders to come, we are called to a route along which adversity and relief, troubled waters and plain sailing, affliction and healing are as part of life as night and day. We live in 'in-between' times, where both the legacy of a fallen world and the foretaste of a new and glorious kingdom intermingle. Most of us would rather not have the mixture, but there it is.

It is here that the coming, living, dying and rising again of Christ can speak volumes to us as we try to cope with our infirmities. God is a God who entered into the old, disintegrating order to bring his kingdom on earth. In his Son, he experienced, first hand, hunger, thirst, weariness, discomfort and the appalling sequence of the Passion, in order to bring us hope and victory. Jesus 'for the joy set before him endured the cross', and we are to 'fix our eyes on him' (Heb 12:2). God, in Christ, suffers with us in our sufferings; God, in Christ, rejoices with us in our healings, our anticipations of the joy and glory 'set before' us.

Jung once said, 'Nothing is more unbearable for the patient than to be always understood,' except, we might add, to be always *mis*understood. I hope that none whose stories contribute to these pages do feel misunderstood by what I have written. The attempt, throughout, has been to be fair to the essence of their accounts, though details have often needed to be altered to obscure people's identities. I trust I will be forgiven if I have, inadvertently, offended any sensitivities.

It is difficult for me to be specific in the many acknowledgments I would like to make. The gathering of the stories told has been through questionnaires, interviews and other personal contacts. I am grateful to those who have helped in collecting the material, but cannot mention them by name lest confidence be breached. I would also like to thank the many who have been willing to share their experiences. I know that this has been a painful enterprise for some and I am all the more appreciative of their honesty and integrity. Such, in giving something of themselves, will, I am sure, encourage many who are caught up with illness or disability, dying or death itself.

Roger F. Hurding

1

OUT OF THE BLUE

I was struck all of a heap
                              Sheridan

Health is a great twentieth century preoccupation. We have
an almost unhealthy interest in health! In an age that knows
so much about the human body most of us see health as our
birthright. Expectant mothers do their best with diet, rest and
exercise to bring healthy babies into the world. A great deal
of normal parental concern is felt whenever a child becomes
ill; by the same token, there is much relief when the fever,
cough or rash is over and the little one is once more alert and
bright-eyed. Most parents take it as read that their teenage
offspring will not be seriously ill. Adolescents, whether they
are lazy or industrious, lethargic or energetic, are expected to
be basically healthy. Appendicitis or glandular fever are seen
as unwelcome interruptions to the flow of exams or job-
hunting.

Whether working or unemployed, married or single,
divorced or widowed, many adults settle into routines of
getting or keeping fit. These routines are often intermittent
though well-intended: bouts of jogging, cycling, press-ups,
chest-expanding, running on the spot; enthusiasms for
aerobics, popmobility and other dance 'work-outs'; concerns
about the latest views on vitamins, food additives and diet.
Muscles are built up, layers of fat are lost in this quest for
fitness and the body beautiful. The years slip by, contours

become pear-shaped but the trim figure is still admired. Squash might be replaced by golf, jogging by stepping out with a walking stick, but the desire for a healthy frame is still with us. Given the choice, most would rather die 'with their boots on' – painting the house, digging the garden, visiting a neighbour or walking the dog.

In spite of today's health-consciousness, most of us, much of the time, take our health for granted. Our bodies function normally in every respect. When we open our eyes in the morning we can see the room around us and the view from the window: colours, light, shade, shape and texture all present their correct value. Though with mixed feelings, we hear the alarm clock, the baby crying or the factory hooter; if our ears are trained, we also pick up the sound of jackdaws calling on the roof or a robin singing in the garden. The noises and sounds of the day, welcome and unwelcome, are before us. Our sense of smell is also awake to the aromas of the day ahead: frying bacon, percolating coffee, wet earth, petrol fumes, cigarette smoke, the local brewery, polished floors, washing powder, perfume, freshly mown grass. We sleep well, our appetites are good, we enjoy the taste of our favourite foods, we can bend to tie our shoe-laces or pick up a fork, we can reach up to open a window or lift down a dish, we can stand, sit or lie-down without pain, we can run for a bus if we need to. While we work, relax or sleep, the body's intricate functions do their job: the heart pumps efficiently, breathing aerates the circulation at just the right rate, the digestive processes make nourishment available and the glands keep hormone levels constant.

All this is, quite sensibly, taken for granted – for after all, we have lives to live and it would be counterproductive to become frequent checkers of pulse-rates and lung movements. And yet, those of us with health on our side would do well, from time to time, to stop, observe and thank God for our senses, mobility and strength. We might say, in the words of Psalm 139:14, 'I praise you because I am fearfully and wonderfully made.'

What, however, of those who, perhaps after years of

uninterrupted good health, become seriously ill? Suddenly or gradually, what has generally been accepted as their due becomes a thing of the past. The body which, in its well-being, has been a pleasant companion or a willing servant becomes, in the face of illness, a traitor or a taskmaster: the ill can feel let down or held down by their unwellness. Let us, in this chapter, consider the situation where the formerly fit meet acute illness 'out of the blue'.

Facing Acute Illness

Jonathan was an all-rounder. He read Law at Oxford and worked as a successful barrister in the south of England. Tall and well built, he had represented the university in the modern pentathlon, an event for the versatile where skills of riding, shooting, fencing, swimming and cross-country running are tested. He was a popular figure, had a wide range of friends of all ages and both sexes and moved easily within many different social circles. His deeply held Christian faith, further training and ordination as a non-stipendiary minister in the Church of England were enhanced by his sense of fun and infectious laughter. This brilliant young man was in his prime when, in his late twenties, he was faced with the diagnosis of a particularly virulent form of skin cancer. When asked, a year or so after the pathology was established, how he had first felt on becoming ill, he replied, 'I was deeply shocked and incredulous. I rejected the possibility that anything serious would follow.' Within the same year, Jonathan married Kate, a newly trained nurse who was also a qualified illustrator. It was not until medical evidence showed that the cancer had spread that Kate 'began to realise the awful reality of the situation', as she put it.

This element of shock and disbelief is one of a number of reactions that fit people face when they are told of the potential seriousness of their condition. Such numbness is part of the mind's defence against Kate's 'awful reality'. No one in his or her right mind wants to be told, 'You are

seriously ill' or, 'You have a fatal illness.' The doctor's words
might be heard but their significance is resisted tooth and
nail. It is this understandable reluctance to admit an
unwelcome diagnosis that can make friends and relatives
want to guard themselves and others from the slowly
dawning truth. In conversation with Kate, during a grim few
days when Jonathan's disease had taken a turn for the worse,
she shared with me the anguish of telling others how bad
things were for her newly wed husband: 'Every person I
tell... it makes it all more definite.' It was hearing herself tell
others that he now had secondaries and the outlook was
bleak that stirred Kate's numbness into unwelcome life. He
really was dying and that admission would bring many
untold pains.

Though the first reaction to such bad news may be one of a
numbing disbelief, in time the reality of the situation may
lead to the predominance of fear. (Anger too can become a
prevailing emotion and we will pick up with its complexity at
a number of points throughout the book.) Resistance to what
the doctors say, or imply, gives way to a realisation of
possible implications. At one end of the scale, there may be
quite simply a degree of apprehension about immediate
practicalities: the readjustment of a job, the cancelling of a
holiday, the adapting to a few weeks in hospital.

In the autumn of 1978 I finally lost all serviceable vision in
my remaining 'good eye' after a year or two of progressive
blindness due to longstanding diabetes.[1] At that stage I was
not to know that sight in the same eye would be restored by
two operations during the next eighteen months. We were on
holiday in the Lake District at the time and, while my wife
Joy drove us home, my concern was not primarily with the
far-reaching implications of a life with little useful vision, so
much as with the problems of being unable to attend to my
patients on the following Monday and of needing to find
another speaker to take my place at a forthcoming meeting.
Perhaps it is a mercy that the more long-term aspects of acute
and serious illness are often, to start with, hidden from view
by day-to-day adjustments.

However, fears for the future may become more deep-seated and threatening: Will I have much pain? If so, how will I cope? Will the doctors and nurses try to relieve the pain? Will they succeed? Will I become an invalid? If so, how will I manage? Will I be a burden to others? Will family and friends find me 'too much'? Is this condition fatal? If so, will I die soon? What will dying be like? Where will I be when I die? Will I die alone? and, perhaps most poignant for many: How will those nearest me manage when I die?

Let us, then, look at these profounder fears under three broad headings: *What will happen to me? What will happen to them?* and *What is happening to them now?* Some of these themes will be picked up again in later chapters.

1.   What will happen to me?

(a) Dependency

There is a Danish proverb which declares, 'Sickness is every man's master.' When faced with sudden and grave illness, one of the deepest of human fears is a loss of freedom, the need to submit to the mastery of sickness. Imagine a fit and active man in his mid-thirties. Let us say that he is ambitious, has worked his way up to positions of increasing responsibility and is now at his peak, ready to go anywhere and take on anything to further his career. In the midst of his successes, his wife persuades him to seek medical advice for some difficulty in swallowing and his recent tendency to drop things. It seems trivial enough but, in time and with the advent of other symptoms, he is told that he has motor neurone disease and is likely to become confined to a wheelchair within a year or two. Imagine, in turn, a strong and athletic young woman in her late thirties. She has always prized her fitness, keeping trim through squash in the winter, tennis in the summer and jogging regularly throughout the year. She feels she is too tied up in her business, sporting and social lives to go to the doctor with a query about a breast lump. It is the discovery of increasing swelling under the arm that takes her to the surgery and to a diagnosis of breast cancer with secondary growth.

Both this man and woman are in their prime and both are suddenly confronted with a complete about-face in life. Both will keep going as long as they can but the prospects of readjustment, frustration and, possibly, progressive dependence loom ahead. For the man, each step towards the wheelchair may be a crisis of giving up long cherished activity: his job, his driving, his dabbling in DIY, his kicking a ball around with his son. For the woman, after the shock of the diagnosis and her need for surgery and radiotherapy, there may be a slower dawning (if the treatment proves unsuccessful) that she has to give up much in her valued lifestyle. Her robust independence may have to be laid aside for a life which increasingly relies on friends and family.

When I first became blind it was my situation of extreme dependency that was specially hard to adjust to. Initially, I was advised to spend six weeks as inactively as possible in order to prevent further bleeding at the back of the eyes. Joy tracked down a comfortable, second-hand Parker Knoll chair which became my habitation for most of the ensuing eight months of blindness. There were many aspects to my sudden dependence on others for the simplest needs: which, in the pile of cassettes at my side, was the piece by Mozart that I wanted to hear? Or, during mealtime, was the plate I was eating from reasonably clean yet? Or, in the middle of getting dressed, where was the sock that matches the one I had just put on – whichever *that* was?

Behind the frustrations of these practical matters, was the deeper pain of a basic loss of adult freedom. My parents had recently moved from the other side of England to be near us and it was occasionally in their presence that I felt the greatest pangs of deprivation. They, though in their early seventies, were still fit and active and at times were a tremendous help to Joy in terms of routine housework and other jobs that needed doing. For me, in my mid-forties, it was a 'back to childhood' experience with respect to a son's helplessness that did wonders for my male pride!

(b) *Pain*

Like people, pains come in all shapes and sizes: the nagging discomfort of toothache, the tight band of tension headache, the hot throbbing of an abscess, the dull persistent ache of an arthritic hip, the searing colic of acute appendicitis, the vice-like clamp of a heart attack or the excruciating agony of some kidney pains. As Marcel Proust has written, 'Illness is the doctor to whom we pay most heed . . . pain we obey.' It is only the masochist who actually enjoys pain. Some pains can be ignored, but there comes a point for all of us beyond which pain can become intolerable. It demands attention. Where it is strong and shouts loudest we have to 'obey' it by taking heed, seeing advice and looking for relief.

However, for others the worst pain is the pain anticipated. It is the fear that discomfort might be too much to cope with that particularly undermines. It is this apprehension that is often behind anxiety about operations and other surgical procedures. Will it hurt? Will it be more than I can bear? Will they realise I'm in pain? Will I be able to call for help? These fears are deep-seated and may go back to some childhood situation of panic in the face of pain, real or imagined. One man in his late thirties, Andrew, a Christian minister, admitted to a long-standing dread of 'all things surgical' and found one of the worst things in his own recent illness related to the anticipation of an abdominal operation.

(c) *Death*

For some, the greatest fear at the onset of acute, serious illness is not the prospect of being bed-bound, assigned to a wheelchair, operated on or in pain so much as the anticipation of death. There is nothing more final than death and few of us, whether in our twenties or eighties, are prepared for such finality. A sudden coronary, a stroke, a diagnosis of cancer or AIDS may bring what we know will happen one day (for most of us, we feel, a very distant 'one day') alarmingly close.

There are some opposing reasons for this fear. For many –

especially the young, the successful, the contented – the response to imminent death is, 'Not yet, please'. Life is very good at the moment and promises well for many a year ahead. We catch this element of 'not yet, please' in Psalm 102:24 where the afflicted psalmist cries out, 'Do not take me away, O my God, in the midst of my days.' There is something in all of us that objects strongly when the young and talented face death. We feel keenly the waste of a life of promise where so much of value seems to be forfeited. There was something of this perfectly reasonable outrage in Jonathan's reaction to his own crippling cancer when he wrote, 'I feared death and separation from my wife-to-be and family and friends. I was angry and questioned God why I had been chosen to suffer.'

Whereas for Jonathan the tragedy of approaching death lay in its prematurity and in the loss of countless opportunities for good, there are others for whom the timing of death will never be right. It is of these that Paul wrote in 1 Corinthians 15:56, 'The sting of death is sin, and the power of sin is the law.' For such, death is always unwelcome because life has not been lived aright. Years spent with backs turned on God do not make for a readiness to face him beyond the grave. Such have not found the death-defying perspective of Paul's next verse, 'But thanks be to God! He gives us the victory through our Lord Jesus Christ.'

2. What will happen to them?

One of the greatest concerns that press in on those who are seriously ill is how will those left behind cope if the illness should prove fatal. This anxiety is often strongest in the acute phase of a potentially lethal disease – at a stage when friends and family have not had chance to prove their worth as copers. The level of the patient's concern will also vary with exactly who will be left bereaved – whether, for example, it will be a young family whose father has already died; a competent and fit wife where the children are now grown up and supportive; parents who are together and mutually caring; or an eighty-year-old husband who lives in a residential home. In all situations there is likely to be apprehension in the one who anticipates death, but the degree of fear will be less where the loved ones that will remain are well provided for.

I am reminded here of two women whose children were still young and dependent on their parents. Facing a fatal condition is perhaps never more heartbreaking than where a caring and competent mother becomes seriously ill and has the prospect of leaving her brood behind. Judy was an efficient young mum who loved her children dearly and, because her husband Giles had a busy office job and often worked late, was a pivotal influence in the family. Her first reaction when told that she had cancer was one of panic – not primarily because of what might happen to her but because of all the implications for her husband's career and children's nurture. The initial fears were lessened through Giles' supportive care and their conviction of God's protective love.

Like Judy, Fiona was a young mother when she faced the strong probability of cancer. Throughout the night before an exploratory operation she was kept awake by thoughts of her husband and three children. What worries she had for their lives without her she was able, in the small hours, to face and turn into a letter to each of them. This looking into the unknown enabled her to commit her loved ones, individually, into the safe keeping of their wise and loving Father. She found peace, and sleep, in handing over her wholly understandable anxieties to the Lord.

However, it has to be said that, in the midst of acute illness, our concern for those we might have to leave behind is not always as honourable as the mother-love shown by Judy and Fiona. One of the most harrowing (and ultimately enriching) aspects of being on the receiving end of a fatal affliction is a realisation of how mixed our seemingly worthy motives are. Further, it is probably fair to say that how we view life for the friends and relatives who will survive us is a pretty accurate mirror of how we have handled relationships with them before our illness. Strangely, it is those who dominate others in everyday life and those who are the most diffident that have the particular common ground of unease about those left behind. It is the over confident and the under confident who may worry that the bereaved *will* cope and, thereby, prove that the one who has died is dispensable after all. To be aware of our own sullied motives at this point can add greatly to the turmoil of adjustment for the seriously ill person. Let us consider these two extremes in turn.

There are many marriages in which one partner or the other predominates, where one is more powerful, tends to be more decisive and usually has the last word. Traditionally, it has been the man who has been seen to be dominant. There have always been exceptions to this pattern, though in the past acceptance of a wife's ascendancy in an observed marriage has often been grudging. The commonplace, 'Guess who's wearing the trousers!' has frequently been accompanied by a nudge and a knowing wink. In today's marriages there is usually a readier acknowledgment that a woman's personality and experience may lead to a greater influence within a partnership than her husband's. The real point here, though, is not so much the existence of a stronger spouse, be it husband or wife, so much as that that strength may lead to over dependence on the part of the other.

Marriages like this function well as long as the strong one remains strong. Where, for example, a husband manages the household like a well-run business and makes all the decisions, his wife's compliance is unchallenged while he stays competent. If we find that, in the event of him contracting a fatal illness, he still insists on holding the reins we may wonder what thought he has for his wife's survival following his death. Such over-control may reveal the husband's need to subdue others and his own unwillingness to accept that his wife can take initiatives and see them through. No wonder he fears that she might cope after he has died!

Another set of complicated emotions may come into play when a person of low self-esteem anticipates death. Let us take the example of a woman who has always been unsure of herself. She has, perhaps, made some progress within her marriage to a caring husband. His affection has encouraged her to value herself more – not least in feeling that he really needs her. Suddenly, she is told she has a malignant disease. Within the marriage she has begun to carve out her indispensability to both husband and children – and now she has to confront leaving them to their own devices. If her self-acceptance is still precarious it will be hard for her to see that they can cope, even when she is laid low. There may be a deep fear within that her family will rise up following her death and manage really rather well. This worry may be made worse by the thought that the husband might re-marry, finding someone whose competence will cast his first wife in a poor light.

3. What is happening to them now?

When a friend becomes seriously ill, our immediate reflex is to reach out in love to that individual, to try to understand what is going on and how he or she is managing. This automatic concern is entirely to the point. However, there is a danger of so focusing our attention on the person who is ill that we spare little thought for the others who are caught up in the drama. What of the flatmate who suddenly sees a lifelong friend in distress, the fiancée who faces the loss of one with whom life promised so much, the father who has to watch his daughter die of leukaemia, the wife who anticipates long months of nursing a fractious, pain-ridden husband or an elderly son who sees his mother half-paralysed by a stroke?

In many ways, what happens to the patient is mirrored in the reaction of those nearest and dearest. We have already seen how Jonathan and Kate experienced an initial numbness when they heard of his cancer. There was a mutual sense of shock, and yet there he still was – full of humour, in spite of it all, and as strong as an ox. It is small wonder that the medical diagnosis left them with a feeling of incredulity. It was a similar experience for David when, in his mid-twenties, he learned that his girlfriend, Sharon, had secondaries following cancer of the breast. Sharon 'found it hard to believe' that she was in danger and David admitted to 'disbelief, followed by a two week period of much fear'.

It is natural that the first shock felt when a loved one is declared to be seriously ill is followed by a range of negative emotions. As reality sinks in, the implications of the illness for the future have to be faced. How will we manage? Will I be equal to what might be demanded of me? How will I cope if my loved one is out of action? Who will support me if it all gets too much? Questions like these are completely appropriate but, because they are usually unanswerable, they often lead to fear and anxiety. David, following his disbelief at Sharon's diagnosis of further cancer, went through a 'two week period of much fear'. Later, when they married, this fear recurred, particularly at night when he felt anxious about whether he would be able to help her if she was in bad pain or vomiting. Understandably, apprehension increased when his shift-work kept him away at night. The fear of his not coping while present gave way to the fear of her not coping while he was absent.

Fear and anger can be either side of the same coin. Where fear is a shrinking back from what might be, anger is an aggressive advance toward what is perceived. Anger is fear that has taken courage. It is not unusual for those close to the sufferer to experience a sequence of numbness, fear and anger. Kate, as the awful truth that her beloved Jonathan was dying of cancer dawned on her, wrestled with 'dark moods of anger and feeling intolerant with people'. By now the couple had married and the sheer unreasonableness of their situation weighed down on her. It is no wonder that she felt 'hard-done-by' for, in fact, she *was* 'hard-done-by'. Her fears for the future were coupled with anger at the present as she watched her young husband suffer.

Coping with Acute Illness

When you or I are faced with the sudden onset of serious illness, how are we to react? Some people seem to go to pieces.

They appear to take the doubtful advice:

> When in trouble, when in doubt,
> Run in circles, scream and shout.

Others battle on stoically and yet find no solution to their suffering, allowing the numbness, fear and anger to fossilise into a hardened and often bitter view of life. This attitude was well portrayed by Somerset Maugham in *The Moon and Sixpence,* the story of the artist, Charles Strickland, based on the life of Paul Gaugin. In a scene early in the book the narrator is in conversation with Mrs Strickland, the artist's long abandoned wife and now a successful business woman. She seems cold towards her spendthrift husband and, reluctantly, offers to send him a 'certain sum of money'. The writer reflects on her hardness:

> I knew it was not kindness that prompted the offer. It is not true that suffering ennobles the character; happiness does that sometimes, but suffering, for the most part, makes men petty and vindictive.[2]

Some though, who face affliction, find a way through – a way of not only enduring adversity but rising above it. They too, both carers and cared for, experience numbness, fear and anger but, somehow, they also discover a path of blessing. For such there are many strands that contribute to their route forward. These include an *honest praying* which brings hope, the *support of others* which encourages faith and a practical *thinking ahead* born out of love. The negative states of numbness, fear and anger can be lived through and overcome by the growth of faith, hope and love.

1. Honest praying

The story of King Hezekiah is instructive. This king of Judah was outstanding in zeal. Like David long before him, 'He did what was right in the eyes of the Lord' (2 Ki 18:3). During his

reign the temple was purified, the covenant renewed and the
Passover feast reinstated (2 Ch 29–30). In the prime of his life,
he was struck down by a fatal degree of blood poisoning from
an untreated abscess. At the age of about thirty-nine, on
hearing Isaiah's words 'you will die; you will not recover', this
godly achiever 'turned his face to the wall', 'prayed to the
Lord' and 'wept bitterly' (2 Ki 20: 2,3). There was no doubt as
to how heartfelt his prayers were. He recalls how his 'eyes
grew weak' as he looked heavenwards, crying 'I am troubled;
O Lord, come to my aid!' (Isa 38:14).

If, as we face acute illness in ourselves or others, we are to
turn to God in prayer then our pleading must be not only
singleminded but honest. If we are to look painful or fatal
disease in the eye and find the Lord's solace in our time of
need, we have to do something with our perplexity, fear and
anger. The safest and wisest thing is to tell God. Hezekiah did
just this. As we have seen, his reflex on hearing of the deadly
outcome of his sickness was prayer. These were not routine
requests. He was *in extremis* and cried out with the boldness
of a desperate man. He was both complaining and accusing
toward God.

Firstly, Hezekiah records the questioning and complaining
tones of his dialogue with God, 'In the prime of my life must I
go through the gates of death and be robbed of the rest of my
years?' (Isa 38:10). What a reasonable complaint that is for
someone who, at the top of his or her career and at a stage
when new ideas and the strength to effect them are most
available, is suddenly struck down. One day, the machinery
of living is running smoothly, the next, life is at a standstill.

Further, Hezekiah blames God for his demise, 'I waited
patiently till dawn, but like a lion he broke all my bones; day
and night you made an end of me' (Isa 38:13). However we
understand the mystery of suffering (and we will consider this
more fully in chapter three), the Bible seems to teach that, at
times, God at least permits affliction to assail his people. In
the face of this assault, the king declares that the Almighty
had dealt with him as crushingly and comprehensively as a
lion that mauls its prey.

I know that Jonathan and Kate had this sense of outrage at a God who, on occasions, seemed (and the language is mine not theirs) as predatory as a carnivorous beast. They were young, strong, well qualified in their chosen professions, enjoying God's world and serving him faithfully. What more did he want of them? There seemed as little sense in the descent of a lethal, wasting disease on Jonathan's active life as there might be to a healthy zebra singled out by a marauding lion. This feeling of God's destructiveness, echoing Hezekiah's complaint 'day and night you made an end of me', is an experience that many have had as they faced affliction. It is, of course, only one of the many ways we can view God in the midst of our suffering and we will try to see this perspective in its fuller light in later chapters.

Nonetheless, this degree of openness with God seems to be essential if our prayer in the face of adversity is to have any cutting edge. Many of us need to see that it is *perfectly acceptable for us to express to God just how we feel*. It is as we declare to the Lord our warring emotions that he meets us in the turmoil and brings us hope. In time, we may be enabled to say, with Hezekiah, 'Surely it was for my benefit that I suffered such anguish' (Isa 38:17).

2. Support of others

When serious or fatal illness assails a loved one we both seek to reach out to help and, at the same time, look to others for support. Our hope, to be the comfort to a sick relative or friend that we want to be, lies in our receiving help and encouragement from other people.

The story of Elijah is relevant here. He brings unexpected strength into the lives of a widow and her small son as they, due to months of drought, face a lingering death from starvation (1 Ki 17). Elijah proves to be a most welcome 'paying guest'. Her own generous hospitality – even as she anticipates her very last meal – opens up God's provision of a jar of flour and a jug of oil which will go on meeting their needs until the rains come.

When, later, her son dies from an acute and rapidly advancing illness, she turns to her lodger in anger and grief, 'What do you have against me, man of God? Did you come to remind me of my sin and kill my son?' Elijah, the man of God, is a tower of strength to her. His gentle managing of the situation is exemplary. Carrying the boy in his arms up to the guestroom, Elijah lays him on the bed, stretches himself out on the body three times and cries to the Lord, 'O Lord my God, let this boy's life return to him!' His compassionate and identifying manner of praying is effective and the widow knows the joy of holding her living son once more. Whether or not Elijah's lying on the child helped revive him through body warmth, or even artificial respiration, is perhaps less the point than his complete identification, or 'being with', the boy in his need. In fact, human support is here an extension of divine mercy. The mother tells Elijah, 'Now I know that you are a man of God and that the word of the Lord from your mouth is the truth.'

We see many more examples throughout the Bible where the loving support of friends and relatives leads to God's blessing in the life of the sufferer. The roof-dismantling zeal of the men who brought the paralytic to Jesus (Mark 2), the great faith of the centurion in Capernaum on behalf of his paralysed servant (Mat 8) and the quick-witted urgency of the Canaanite woman seeking release for her demon-possessed daughter (Mat 15) illustrate the links between the faith and faithfulness of those who love us and the comfort and healing we receive.

Many of those closest to sick people have shared with me that their own ability to cope hinges on the loving care shown by others. Sonia, a woman in her thirties, the mother of a toddler and expecting her second child, reminisced on her husband's recent illness. She described something of the support she had received in these breathless words: '... meals were brought, ironing done, daughter happily taken care of, (I was) driven to hospital for visiting... mother came for a few days... doctor checking that I and baby were OK... church providing "live in" mother's help for first month of convalescence'. As a result, to use her words again, all this 'meant I could care for my husband instead of the other way round'. In this experience, Sonia acknowledged 'God's continuous presence' in the provision of people and practical help just when they were needed.

3.   Thinking ahead

Just as hope can be experienced by the sufferer as he or she turns to God in honest prayer and faith can be stimulated by close friends and relatives as they both support and are supported, so those who are left behind when an illness proves fatal can know they are loved through sensitive and practical provision.

Perhaps the supreme example of concerned thinking ahead is found in the crucifixion scene. Jesus, hanging on the cross, noticed a handful of the women who loved him standing nearby, with John in attendance. Amongst them he saw Mary, his mother. We read (Jn 19:26,27) that Jesus 'said to his mother, "Dear woman, here is your son," and to the disciple, "Here is your mother." From this time on, this disciple took her into his home.'

This is an arrangement that made a great deal of sense in that John seems to have come from a reasonably well-to-do family. His father, Zebedee, had 'hired servants' and Salome, assumedly John's mother, was one of the women who provided for Jesus 'out of their means' (Mk 1:20; 15:40; Lk 8:3, RSV). Further, the slight variations between the Gospel accounts of the women who witnessed Christ's death suggest that John's mother was in fact Mary's sister and, therefore, Jesus and John were cousins (see Mat 27:56; Mk 16:1; Jn 19:25).

This commital of Mary to John and John to Mary by their dying Lord is echoed, however dimly, in all loving attempts to provide for the future of those left behind. Such care includes, of course, the making of a will, the clearing of debts and the attempt to leave adequate means of support. A legacy of uncertainty about possessions, property and money can be a cruel aftermath to months or years of devotion towards an ill relative.

However, there are many other aspects to helping the carers face the coming days without their loved ones. Sometimes these aspects concern the smaller details of everyday life. For Kate and Jonathan it was the knowledge that the fabric of their rural setting required Kate's co-operation, in the twice-daily milking of their cow, the caring for some newly acquired lambs and the feeding of ducks and chickens, which helped prepare her to carry on the work after his eventual death. In another example, Stephen, a busy professional in his late fifties, faced the rapid physical decline of his wife Margaret. As in many households there was a marked division of labour between them. One of the areas that had always been her priority was that of gardening. Life had to go on, and the need for weeds to be dug out, roses pruned and borders tended continued during her illness. It was an important learning process for Stephen and imparting experience for Margaret when, on one or two occasions, she was strong enough to spend some time in a chair in the garden supervising his attempts at horticulture.

As in Jesus's seal of approval on John and Mary and their subsequent support for each other, so the greatest hope for many as they face the possibility of bereavement is in other people. We all need the love and care of friends and the sort of friends who will stand by us in illness and loss are of inestimable worth. Paul Tournier, the Swiss doctor and author, experienced the deaths of his parents within the first six years of his life. When in his eighties, he wrote that he could see his writings as 'a long search for maternal tenderness'. In that search, his relationships with his wife, Nelly, and a number of key friends have sustained him through times of doubt and pain.[3] He has emphasised the universal need for friendship in these words: 'No one can develop freely in this world and find a full life without feeling understood by at least one person.'

On the other hand, there are times when the commitment of friendship is a burden. Lord Samuel, writing in the *Sunday*

Telegraph in the late 1970s, declared, 'A friend in need is a friend to be avoided'! Sometimes the needs of those we know and love are so overwhelming that we are tempted to be 'unavailable'. This is where a group of people can share the load so effectively. John and Mary had each other, following their Lord's death, but we also see them as part of a band of caring men and women, united in their love for the risen Christ. After the Ascension, the disciples assembled in an upper room in Jerusalem. We read: 'Those present were Peter, John, James and Andrew... They all joined together constantly in prayer, along with the women and Mary the mother of Jesus, and his brothers' (Ac 1:13,14).

Joy and I belong to a group of four couples who, originally, came together as a planning committee for evangelistic outreach. We still arrange, from time to time, supper parties to which we invite our friends so that they may hear and respond to speakers on a wide range of subjects – from adolescence to the Arts, from the media to the Middle East. In planning these ventures we have been drawn together so that we also meet regularly – simply to be together, to listen and share. Through the years we have found mutual support in the joys and pains of everyday life. There have been times of illness, family concern and financial crisis that we have been able to weather, strengthened by the love and prayers of one another. We try to get away as a group for a weekend or two a year. On one of these, during one of our leisurely walks (we all, in some measure or other, feel the challenges of middle age!), a few of us began to discuss the future and the probability of at least one death amongst us within the next few years. We were thinking ahead sensitively and felt assured that whoever was bereaved would continue to know the practical solidarity of us all.

However, for many who face illness life can be very lonely. Those in such isolation include single people of all ages who, for one reason or another, find it difficult to make or keep friends. Others may be more socially adept but circumstances have tended to cut them off from the support they long for. For some, separation, divorce or bereavement can make serious illness almost impossible to bear; for others, the gradual loss of friends and family through the years has led to a loneliness which is simply compounded by the loss of health. One elderly widow I know, for example, finds the prospect of phoning for the doctor, attending Out-Patients, keeping to medical advice and generally coping with pain, loss of appetite and overall unwellness, too daunting to take in her stride. Formerly, all the inconvenience and discomfort of dealing with illness was managed through the daily caring and practical help of a husband who loved her.

For those ill people who live alone, or are tied to elderly parents, the onus is on both the sufferer and on those around who, with more imagination and determination, could be more supportive. Sometimes the unwell person is one who chooses to live in fierce independence and will put up every conceivable barrier to exclude a helping hand. Nonetheless, most people, even amongst those who appear grudging and ungrateful, respond to genuine neighbourliness. Where the help offered is thought out and realistic, whether from the people next door, through a 'street warden' scheme or from caring members of the local church, such practical love can become a lifeline to those who face sickness alone. Where the efforts of good neighbours or voluntary helpers are supplemented by the provision of Meals on Wheels, the attendance of a home help and the regular visits of community nurse, health visitor and doctor, then the trials of being laid aside through acute illness can at least be offset. Where the receiving of everyday care from others is under-girded by an awareness of God's nearness and strengthening then the needy can begin to find the ache of loneliness giving way, at least at times, to the joy and peace of solitude. As Henri Nouwen writes:

> A lonely person has no inner time nor inner rest to wait and listen. He wants answers and wants them here and now. But in solitude we can pay attention to our inner self. This has nothing to do with egocentrism or unhealthy introspection because, in the words of Rilke, 'what is going on in your innermost being is worthy of

your whole love.' In solitude we can become present to ourselves... Solitude does not pull us away from our fellow human beings but instead makes real fellowship possible.[4]

Some final thoughts

Acute illness that comes to us 'out of the blue' is unsettling and unwelcome. Fortunately, sickness that can come suddenly can also leave suddenly! The natural history of many medical conditions, even of a serious nature, is one of clearing up in time. As we have seen, the experience of affliction, through prayer, support and thinking ahead, can be the context for increased hope, rekindled faith, the deepening of human affection and a new outpouring of God's love. Andrew, the Christian minister mentioned earlier, looked back at several months of harrowing illness with these words:

> The experience was very special in terms of being reduced to the state of simple obedience. I quite hanker after that... As one who has feared all things surgical it has given me greater sensitivity in being with the sick and the dying. I believe that the Spirit through this has gifted me to minister to such.

Andrew has been able to leave his time of sickness behind but can still reflect on God's special grace in and through his hour of need. In the next chapter we will seek to trace a positive way forward in the face of illness that will not go away. Can God bless there too?

2

NOT STILL ILL!

The world gets better every day – then worse again in the evening

Frank McKinney Hubbard

It had been one of those glorious Indian Summer days. Joy and I were spending five days on Colonsay, a ten-mile-long island thirty miles out from Oban on the Scottish west coast. It was October 1979 and we had looked forward to a break for some time. I had emerged, five months before, from a long winter of blindness alleviated by an operation on my right eye. As my one-sided sight improved, our fifteen-year-old son, Simon, and I had been stricken by a puzzling, feverish condition that took many months to diagnose. Eventually, it was established that we had caught brucellosis, or undulant fever, from some soft cheese he had brought back from France at Easter. Fortunately, Simon's immune system defeated the bug after two months' illness, but my own 'sub-standard' diabetic body seemed unable to resist and my recurring flu-like state continued. However, I now had some restored vision, certain friends had paid for our Motor-Rail to Scotland and we were ensconced on a beautiful Hebridean island, staying in its one hotel in a room looking out across the water to the hills of Jura. God had been good to us and we luxuriated in the pleasant tiredness that followed a day of autumnal sunshine exploring the coves, promontories and sand-dunes of the south-west coast.

We slept well that night, keenly anticipating a proposed

visit the next day to Kiloran Bay and its rocky hinterland, where, so we had been told, we might see golden eagles. Apart from a sleepy walk to the loo in the small hours, I did not wake till 7.00 a.m. Joy was still asleep. It felt very good lying there, reminding myself just where we were and what we would do over the coming day or two. These plans were short-lived. As I opened my eyes the room swirled in a misty blackness. I closed them again, trying to persuade myself that I still dreamed. It was no good. I was definitely awake: I could feel Joy's back pressed against mine, the sheets and blankets moulding my painfully alert body. It was some time before I risked another glance across the room. As I did so, the awful truth was established that there had been a heavy retinal bleed in the right eye and I faced a future of blindness once more.

Joy and I breakfasted in our bedroom that morning, choked and silent. Later, we found our way, still speechless, a half mile or so down to the island's jetty. From there we wandered over the rough moorland that skirts the eastern seaboard. In time, we stood together in the wind and wept.

After lunch, Joy drove us to a favourite spot on the *machair* (the close-cropped, springy turf of the west coast) where we sat in the car and listened to the waves. The impossible numbness of the dawn was giving way to anger. Fear and foreboding were there too, but after a previous eight months' blindness the implications of a life of very limited vision were well known. It was anger that predominated. What was God up to? Why bring us on a long and exhausting journey to a remote Scottish island, the cost backed by generous friends, and then, after just one wet day and one fine day, blot the landscape out in a stroke? What was he trying to teach us? We had, by his grace, survived a long stretch of being 'laid aside': first the blindness, then the onset of brucellosis. Why this third 'lesson'? The angry questions darted to and fro in our minds, occasionally bursting through into tearful words.

Anger is just one of the negative responses we can have to recurring or unremitting illness. Just as numbness, fear and the seeds of anger often make up our reaction to affliction 'out of the blue', so anger, anxiety or depression can be the upshot of long-term disease. Sometimes the latter three are linked, the toxic effects of an *anger* that is nursed including a crippling form of *anxiety*, where unresolved inner conflicts make life seem a very threatening place; and *depression*, in which feelings of rage are allowed to fester within.

Before looking at these emotions in detail, it is worth noting that they arise primarily – at least in the case of chronic illness – from a sense of loss. Whether being ill leads to the loss of employment, status, usefulness, acceptability, mobility, sight, hearing or other bodily function, it is important to see that such deprivation can result in a form of grief, or bereavement. These specific losses are often undergirded by a loss of independence (see chapter one) and, paradoxically, a loss of contact with others. In the first, there can be a sensation of being 'taken over', however lovingly, and in the second, a feeling of being 'left out'. These themes of loss will recur throughout this book but, for the moment, let us concentrate on the reactions of anger, anxiety and depression.

Anger

Ernest Becker has said, 'Anger for most people is an alternative to fading away.' Anger is a response to what happens to us or around us. Whether it is for good or ill, in haste or on reflection, expressed or kept within, anger shows the necessity of dealing with what provokes us. The need to respond is part of our humanity. We are not machines or ciphers, but flesh and blood. If we are to keep engaged in everyday life anger cannot be avoided. The only alternative, as Becker indicates, is a 'fading away' – a 'switching off' which, as we shall see, can allow anger to re-surface as anxiety or depression.

Accepting that anger is part and parcel of human existence, let us see something of what the scriptures say about this negative emotion. First and foremost, we realise that anger is a divine attribute. We have a God who responds to human wilfulness in an uncompromising manner: 'for those who are self-seeking and who reject the truth and follow evil, there will be wrath and anger' (Ro 2:8). Both Old and New Testaments speak of the Lord's judgment on sinful humanity in graphic terms. Those who rebel will be forced to drink to the dregs from a cup filled with the 'wine of God's fury'; their resulting drunkenness and degradation will make them an easy prey for divine retribution (see Isa 51:17; Jer 25:15,16; Rev 14:10). Such pictures give a frightening portrayal of God's anger that burns against the persistently disobedient.

However, we must understand that behind divine rage there is divine compassion. The wrath of God has been described as 'an expression of rejected and wounded love'.[1] We observe the close link between a godly sorrow and righteous anger in the life of Jesus. When, for example, his love reaches out to the man with a shrivelled hand, the Lord is both angry at and hurt by those religious Jews who put rules and regulations before human need. We read, 'He looked round at them in anger and, deeply distressed at their stubborn hearts, said to the man, "Stretch out your hand"' (Mk 3:5).

Because we are made in God's image and, as Christians, are being changed into Christlikeness, then godly anger is a clear possibility within our human experience. Examples abound in the Bible. Moses exploded in a violent rage at the people's idolatry (Ex 32:19); David burned with anger at the unjust sufferings of the poor man in Nathan's story (2 Sa 12:5); Nehemiah silenced the nobles and officials with his angry indictment of their oppressive policies (Ne 5:6,7). In the New Testament, injustice is responded to angrily by the kings in the parables of the unmerciful servant and the wedding feast (Mat 18:34; 22:7) and we are urged not to sin in our anger (Eph 4:26).

All this is not to deny that our angry responses are commonly *un*righteous – both in what the anger is responding to and in the way it responds. It was Benjamin

Franklin who said, 'Anger is never without a reason, but seldom with a good one' and we see wrong reasons for anger throughout the pages of Scripture: the jealousy that provoked Cain's murderous rage towards Abel (Ge 4:5); the sense of being cheated that led to Esau's outburst against Jacob (Gen 27:34); Moses' impatience at the waters of Meribah (Ex 17:7; Dt 32:51); the psalmist's awareness of frustration and envy as a source of wrong anger (Ps 37:8); the fool's annoyance at being insulted (Pr 12:16).

Further, the manner in which anger is handled can, in turn, lead to a range of ugly results – including resentment, cruelty, strife, revenge and murder (see, for example, Job 36:13; Pro 27:4; 30:33; 2 Sam 12:20–29; Ge 4:8). Paul, in writing to the Ephesians (4:31), indicates the spread of poison that wrong anger can release, 'Get rid of all bitterness, rage and anger, brawling and slander, along with every form of malice.'

What has all this talk of righteous and unrighteous anger to do with the angry response to loss in persistent illness? What of the speechless rage that gripped Joy and me on Colonsay? How does that fit in with the scriptural perspectives we have just thought about?

Ephesians 4:26 tells us, 'In your anger do not sin' and, as Thomas Secker has stated, 'He that would be angry and sin not must not be angry with anything but sin.' Is it right, then, to be outraged at those *outworkings* of sin and the Fall that spoil people's lives? I believe it is. It seems to me that it is a godly reaction to burn with anger not only at human pride, selfishness and greed but at the tragedies that overtake humanity through natural disaster, economic injustice, repressive or neglectful governments, as well as the vast range of disease – physical and emotional, genetic and acquired, man-caused and fortuitous. The deeply felt opposition that Jesus had to 'all the works of the devil' is a pointer to our need for a holy anger against the destructive effects of sin and sickness.

When we are personally afflicted it is likely that our angry response will be a mixture of good and bad. The reaction that Joy and I had was directed primarily at God – since he was our loving Father and, we felt, was meant to be looking after us! Our anger was a compound of outrage, puzzlement and self-pity because our finite minds could not see any sense or plan in a life that seesawed in and out of blindness. We had grasped something of the character-forming aspect of suffering during the previous year of loss of vision and brucellosis but could not accept, in those first bitter hours, the immediate need for more 'refining' – at least, not during five days' holiday!

Ephesians 4:26 is, in fact, a quotation from Psalm 4:4, which reads:

> In your anger do no sin;
> When you are on your beds,
> search your hearts and be silent.

This verse seems to suggest that there is a profound need to 'hold back' when we become angry – to allow for the stilling effect of quiet reflection in solitude. Joy and I did not wait till we reached our bed at the hotel that night but, as we sat in the car, we were gradually able to keep our peace and listen. Joy read some extracts from Edith Schaeffer's *Affliction* with its helpful theme of the God who is sovereign and who says, 'I will have mercy on whom I have mercy, and I will have compassion on whom I have compassion' (Ro 9:15). While we then kept our silence, we were also reminded that God is no remote arbiter over our lives but a God who suffers with us. A fresh awareness of the identifying love of Christ, 'who stood where we stood', began to dawn. The one who endured the cross 'for the joy set before him' was alongside, and somehow his sufferings encompassed our own. The loss of vision was still there, tears continued to be near the surface but our anger was stilled and peace came slowly upon us.

Anxiety

There are a number of ways of using the words 'anxious' and

'anxiety'. They may express a simple desire: 'I'm anxious to see you again while you're in the area'; an understandable concern: 'I feel anxious when you stay out after midnight without phoning'; a fear of some unpleasant reality: 'I admit I'm really anxious about having tomorrow's big operation'; or a crippling apprehension about what *might* happen, even though there are no reasonable grounds for anxiety: 'I know you're fit, sensible and safe but I just can't help feeling anxious all the time while you're away.' We considered some of the logical fears that can attend serious illness in the last chapter. Let us now think about the way an excessive and unreasonable anxiety can undermine coping with affliction.

Emily, now in her early sixties, is the daughter of a mother who, though in poor health, was uncomplaining and a father who worried continually about his physical condition. Emily grew up with a chronic tendency to anxiety, anticipating trouble at every turn. She became convinced that she was ill and, in spite of numerous investigations and the doctors' reassurance, settled in her mind that she was a long-term sufferer. She modelled her style of managing life on her mother's stoicism, tending to look down at men as non-copers. She eventually married Maurice, a kindly and caring man who worked in a local hardware store. Though Emily continued to move from one anxiety about her health to another, Maurice was not allowed to be ill. If he succumbed to feeling unwell, she would either ignore him or tell him to pull himself together. They had a daughter whom she adored and two sons that she had little time for.

As with many people who suffer from chronic anxiety, and wear others down with their hypochondriasis, Emily 'cried wolf' once too often. Most of her life she had spent calling for help for imagined conditions and now, in her late fifties, and perhaps brought on by habitual tension, she had a heart attack. She received excellent medical and nursing care and a great deal of devotion from Maurice. Although she has recovered well, much of her conversation centres on her 'coronary'. She looks back through the years with a triumphant gleam in her eye, declaring, 'I always knew the doctors were wrong when they told me my trouble was just nerves!'

Here is someone who has worked hard at playing the role of patient. She felt she was following her mother's example of coping with illness – and in a sense she was, except that for most of Emily's life the illness was imagined. Unresolved inner conflicts about her relationships with her parents slowed up her own maturing as a person so that her security rested on being taken seriously as an invalid. It is likely that her anxiety was linked to deeply buried anger towards her non-coping father and, thereby, to any men close to her who threaten to give way to illness. When she finally experienced a serious medical condition she was, in effect, delighted because her life-long commitment to being ill was at last realised. Her hidden anger against male inadequacy had been exonerated. She, as a representative of stoical womanhood, was in the clear.

Emily's story is given as an example of a level of unproductive anxiety which is commonly labelled as an 'anxiety state' or 'anxiety neurosis' by the medical profession. Broadly, its symptoms can be divided into the mental and bodily. Features of the mental state include tension, apprehension, worry and self-doubt, with a strong tendency to anticipate trouble at every turn. The body and the mind intricately affect each other and so it is not surprising that any, or every, system of the body can be upset. Persistently anxious people may experience rapid heartbeats, breathlessness, excessive sweating, difficulty in swallowing, indigestion, constipation, diarrhoea, increasing frequency of passing urine, various muscle and joint aches, weakness of the limbs, as well as feelings of general unwellness, faintness and tiredness. Sometimes the link between anxiety and its bodily expression is more specific and we then talk of 'psycho-somatic' illness. Although, in the past, doctors have seen a close association between tension and certain physical disorders, the complexity of cause and effect is now more fully appreciated. However, conditions like coronary heart disease, some forms of high blood pressure, asthma, duodenal ulcers, certain varieties of colitis and arthritis, migrainous headaches and a wide range of skin diseases, have been seen as having psychosomatic components.

What remedies are there for the anxiety states that lie behind so much recurring illness? The level of worry that Emily exhibited had its seeds, as we have seen, in deep psychological causes and such sufferers may find help through long-term counselling or various forms of psychotherapy. Many are unwilling for that sort of commitment or unable to find the degree of care they would like. Instead, they may find a measure of relief from distressing symptoms, whether mental or bodily, through medication, relaxation exercises or other varieties of behaviour modification. Clearly, where a person suffers from fully developed psychosomatic illness, medical care will need to be open to both psychological and physical factors if substantial help is to be given.

It is as we turn to the Bible that we see that, whatever support we might find in professional help, there are some crucial spiritual aspects of trying to deal with our worrying natures – whether we battle with a chronic anxiety state like Emily's or, more simply, with a tendency to be anxious about everyday things.

As with anger, the scriptures commend right anxiety (concern or care) and condemn wrong anxiety (anxious care). Just as God cares for his Church, the body of Christ, so those to whom he entrusts pastoral responsibility are to care for God's people. Paul, for example, indicates something of the cost of this commitment when he writes, 'I face daily the pressure of my concern for all the churches' (2 Cor 11:28). At another point he hopes to send his 'true son in the faith', Timothy, to the Christians at Philippi and says of him, 'I have no one like him, who will be genuinely anxious for your welfare' (Php 2:20, RSV). In fact, this level of godly caring should be the hallmark of all Church members as they relate to one another:

But God has combined the members of the body and has

given greater honour to the parts that lacked it, so that
there should be no division in the body, *but that its parts
should have equal concern for each other* (1 Cor 12:24,25;
italics mine).

It is this 'equal concern for each other' which can bring the
greatest easing of strain for those who suffer. During the long
periods of blindness I experienced, I was put on the regular
'visiting list' by the staff of Christ Church, Clifton, where Joy
and I worship. The company of these individual Christian
friends was the highlight of each week as we shared, listened
and laughed together. It was not necessarily what was said or
done that was important so much as the 'being with' – the
sense of solidarity and belonging that these visits gave.
Further, the physical presence of these good companions was
supplemented through our cassette recorder – in that a
number of other friends put various short stories and books,
including certain gospels and epistles, on to tape. I thus had
the bonus of listening to familiar voices and feeling a 'cared
for' member of Christ's body at the push of a button.

Although loving concern for the needy is urged upon us in
the scriptures, 'anxious care' is not. It is in the Sermon on the
Mount that we see the clearest teaching which questions a
sinful form of anxiety (Mat 6:25–34). Worry about life's daily
needs is condemned in that it arises from a lack of trust in
God's ability to provide. He looks after the natural order, it is
argued, so why can we not depend on him to care for his
people? Anxious care, Jesus says, is a characteristic of the
godless life and, by implication, a disgrace when found in the
lives of believers. He challenges us all to get it right. The logic
is simple though the application, for many of us, is hard. We
are to put God first in our lives, welcoming his righteous rule
and seeking its extension throughout the world. As we
trustingly obey the Father, he gladly gives us the necessities of
life. We are to meet trouble on a daily basis, not allowing
anxious care about tomorrow to undermine today.

As we face chronic illness in ourselves or in those we love, a
caring concern for one another, as we have seen, is entirely

appropriate. It is as that concern becomes a series of worries, which, in effect, questions God's intention and capacity to care for us, that we go wrong.

For some of us, worrying, as with fear, is tied to this or that particular aspect of our malady; whilst for others, as we saw with Emily, worrying is more diffuse. Duncan Buchanan, in his *The Counselling of Jesus*, helpfully distinguishes between fear and this 'free-floating' anxiety:

> Fear has a focus, anxiety has none, it is a state of worry in which a whole series of 'maybe' or 'perhaps' or 'if only' pervade our attitudes, tying us down and frightening us by their very vagueness. Anxiety is as unspecific as fear is the opposite.[2]

Whether our tendency to worry relates to the fear over specifics that we considered in chapter one or to the vaguer form of anxiety that Buchanan describes, we need to see that 'anxious care' is not only ungodly – it is also unproductive. William R. Inge, the former Dean of St Paul's, London, once said that, 'Worry is interest paid on trouble before it falls due.' It is this unhelpful bringing of the next day's battles into today that is wasteful of both time and energy: an unnecessary conflict which often leaves the anxious tired and listless.

We should all realise, as we try to cope with illness, that chronic anxiety is, at best, an exhausting misuse of human resources and, at worst, a bid for wilful independence. In effect, the language of anxious care is: 'We know best. We do not like the look of what is coming but we insist on making the most of its grim possibilities'! The challenge is clear:

> Humble yourselves, therefore, under God's mighty hand, that he may lift you up in due time. Cast all your anxiety on him because he cares for you (1 Pe 5:6,7).

Depression

As with anger and anxiety, depression has many faces – as indicated by the title of John White's book, *The Masks of Melancholy*.[3] We can talk of depression in terms of mood, attitude, experience and illness.

We all have swings of *mood* which relate in a complex way to the rhythms and cycles of the body's chemistry. We are subject to an inner 'twenty-four hour clock', or circadian rhythm, which affects a pattern of temperature and biochemical change that, in turn, influences how we feel. Globe-trotters know, in addition, the way that disruption of this sequence through jet-lag can upset the most equable dispositions for days. Further, it is well known that the hormonal balance of the menstrual cycle affects the way many women feel, including a tendency for increased irritability, anxiety, hostility or depression during the week before each period. What is not so widely appreciated is that men, too, can be prone to changes in mood which relate to shifts in levels of hormones in the bloodstream. Some of the early research on this matter showed that 60 per cent of the young men investigated had a regular cycle of testosterone, the male hormone, lasting from eight to thirty days. The feelings that accompanied the swing in amounts of hormone were various: high levels of testosterone were equated in some with depression, in others with aggression and, in a third group, with a rise of sexual desire.[4]

Though most if not all of us experience some measure of variation in how we feel, there are some whose basic *attitude* to life is depressed. Those of us who dip in response to our body chemistry may talk of feeling 'flat', 'lifeless', 'fed up', 'browned off', 'down in the dumps', 'cheesed off', 'at a low ebb' or experiencing the 'blues' or 'miseries'. All these terms indicate that we are in a bad patch. However, for the depressive personality life is one long 'bad patch'. There is a fixed pessimism that sees life through black-tinted spectacles. Sometimes this bleakness is lightened by a sense of humour and some of the best quips seem to shine out of a tendency to depression. Woody Allen's one-liners, 'Life is divided up into the horrible and the miserable' and, 'My one regret in life is that I am not someone else' are examples of making light of life's heaviness.

It is on our third and fourth categories of feeling depressed that I want to concentrate with respect to coping with long-term disease: *experience* and *illness*.

First of all, some level of 'feeling down' when facing unwellness is almost inevitable. The loss of independence and function, as we have seen, are bound to lead to some negative reactions – however brave a front we put on the situation. Some medical conditions are particularly prone to a depressive element. Many find this as they try to recover from a bout of flu, and less common illnesses like infective hepatitis, glandular fever, postviral syndrome, brucellosis and Parkinson's disease have a similar tendency. By the same token, those who look after the sick person – with their comparable loss of freedom – may well have stretches of depression. They may be especially inclined to dip in their feelings when the one they are caring for is, they begin to suspect, rather enjoying being an invalid. Maurice, whom we thought about earlier, might well feel increasingly despondent as Emily soars in the triumphant belief that she really is ill and has proved the doctors wrong.

It is where gloomy feelings disrupt the carer's or the patient's everyday functioning that we can begin to talk of depression as *illness*. This is not the place to discuss medical classification in detail but psychiatrists have traditionally divided depressive illness into: reactive, or neurotic, depression, where the condition is provoked by outside circumstances or inner conflict; and endogenous depression (linked with manic-depressive psychosis), where the causation is mainly at the genetic and biochemical levels. Clearly the latter can coincide with physical illness but it is the former that concerns us most in this context.

Reactive depression, as a response to affliction, is usually triggered by the realisation of what negative things the future might hold. Feeling anxious and unhappy, sometimes to the point of hopelessness, the sufferer may be frequently tearful and is often more miserable by the end of the day. There is typically some difficulty in getting to sleep, a loss of concentration and a physical weariness. Such depression may be accompanied by any of a wide range of bodily symptoms, including headaches, chronic back pain and gut problems.

Why is it that one person suffering from an identical disease to another develops a reactive depression whereas the second copes well? Why does one relative 'go to pieces' when faced with caring for an unwell loved one where someone up the road in a parallel situation manages with sensitivity and competence?

Although we may explain different reactions in terms of different external circumstances, there are other theories which look at the depressed person's inner world. A number of these link depression with the dampening down of anger. When the numbness and fear that follow the first announcement of a serious medical condition give way to a sense of outrage, there is always the danger that that anger will not be expressed. This is perhaps where the classic British 'stiff upper lip' can be blamed for a great deal of depression. One young woman, Amy, on hearing that her soldier husband had been killed in the Korean war, decided that she would never show any emotion to her unsympathetic parents. Numbness, fear and anger were unacknowledged and pushed 'out of sight, out of mind'. Sometimes an infection deep in the human body can cause an inflammation which is eventually sealed off by calcification. Amy's negative emotions festered at first and then were gradually surrounded by a hardened shell where only depression could flourish. William Blake pointed to the same process when he wrote, in 'A Poison Tree':

> I was angry with my friend:
> I told my wrath, my wrath did end.
> I was angry with my foe:
> I told it not, my wrath did grow.

At times the anger we suppress is thought by psychologists to have a much earlier origin. It is argued that a baby 'sees' his or her mother as a part of the self and so, where mothering is attentive and caring, a basic trust is built up between parent and infant. When weaning takes place, the child experiences a natural and inevitable element of pain at the withdrawal of the comforting breast. Usually, the bond between mother and baby survives this and a balance is found between her availability to the child and her need to do other things. Sometimes, though, there is a more intense and drawn out 'loss' of the mother where, for example, she is absent due to illness, neglect, a broken marriage or, irrevocably, her death. Her inaccessibility may be just as acute where she is with her child and yet rejects him or her.

Such dislocation, it is said, provokes a rage in the child which it may be quite unacceptable to express. If mother is not there, the baby cries in vain; if she is present and unloving, her harsh voice or rough handling will cow the little one's anger. The sense of outrage is 'kept under wraps' and suppressed.

Later in life, the man or woman who has been through this traumatic loss of maternal love at an early stage will be especially vulnerable at other times of deprivation. It is as if these new situations recapitulate that infantile sense of loss of the loved mother. The anger against being deserted is still there, deeply hidden, and is now masked by the face of depression. Such a theory may explain why some succumb so readily to a depressive illness when they or their loved ones confront serious physical disease, with its attendant losses.

Whether classed as illness or a negative response to adversity, depression of a reactive nature is often completely understandable. Edna and George were in their late fifties when sickness began to upset their lives. She developed a painful condition in her legs which gradually led to a loss of mobility. By the time she had reached her early seventies she was not only chairbound but incontinent. George, working as a postman, found it very difficult to care for her adequately. With retirement, though, he began to devote himself unstintingly to her needs as well as to the general housekeeping. They received great support and much practical help from a rota of district nurses. It is not surprising, regardless of any childhood experiences of deprivation, that Edna should have found her increasing helplessness a harrowing thing to endure. Looking back at how she felt on first becoming ill she replied, 'depressed and frightened' and, in contemplating the future, she said she saw it as 'very bleak', adding 'I wish my life to end'. It is a mark of George's resilience and his ability to cope on her behalf that he declared that he viewed the years ahead 'hopefully'!

As with chronic anxiety, we find that depression is open to a great deal of professional help. Edna is most fortunate to have the level of caring that George provides but she has also received much from community nursing, general practice and the psychiatric services. The reactive form of depression is particularly amenable to psychotherapy, where inner conflicts and a legacy of emotional loss can be explored, understood and come to terms with. This is rarely an easy path since the roots of despair can run so deeply that the individual, especially when facing serious physical illness, readily gravitates to old patterns of negative thinking and behaviour. Such attempts at a 'talking cure' can be supplemented helpfully by antidepressants. Although these drugs have various side-effects, like drowsiness, dry mouth and difficulty in focusing, they can, when taken under close medical supervision, lift the patient's mood and thus ease the often painful venture of psychotherapy.[5]

Let us turn now to the Bible to see whether the basic concepts of family care and professional support for the depressed can be backed up by other God-given principles. We should note, first, two things: on the one hand, the scriptures do not give us a systematic analysis of emotional affliction; on the other hand, they do acknowledge the full spread of feelings and states of mind that men and women experience. Overall, we find a greater emphasis on the 'rejoicing' end of that spectrum than at the 'mourning' end – there being, for instance, roughly four times as many references to joy than to sorrow in the New Testament.[6] It is, in fact, in the Wisdom literature of the Old Testament that we discover the fullest display of what we call today the 'negative' emotions. This is not to deny, too, that the depths of the human predicament are picked up time and again throughout the Bible in the sufferings and death of Jesus Christ.

The most detailed picture in the Bible of an individual's slide into depression is in the story of Job, the man from Uz, who 'was blameless and upright; . . . feared God and shunned evil' (Job 1:1). We have seen how anger and depression, in particular, are often reactions to loss – and the catalogue of deprivation that the story of Job records is formidable: the loss of livestock, servants, sons, daughters and property (Job 1:13–19); looks and health (Job 2:7,8); his wife's respect (Job 2:9); his friends' dependability (Job 6: 14,15); and, profoundest of all, a loss of a sense of God's favour (Job 13:24; 19:7). His physical illness, whatever the precise diagnosis, was vile: he was covered in suppurating, maggot-ridden sores (Job 2:7,8; 7:5); his skin later blackening and peeling (Job 30:30); he was feverish (Job 30:30); his breath smelt foul (Job 19:17); he had nightmares (Job 7:14); he lost weight dramatically (Job 19:20); and his friends could hardly recognise him because of his disfigurement (Job 2:12). John Job, in his *Where is My Father?*, highlights the all-encompassing nature of this malady when he writes: 'Job is an everyman figure and there is a sense in which all our symptoms converge in him.'[7]

It is important for us to see that what Job went through can be, in fact, a source of great encouragement to us in our own afflictions. His story breaks for all time the inevitable link between personal sin and disaster. The Book of Job stresses this man's God-fearing blamelessness and then goes on to portray his sufferings. I draw this point out because many today are forced, often by well-meaning Christian friends, to look for a causal connection between their unwellness and some specific sin in their lives. The association may of course be there (as with Miriam's leprosy in Numbers 12 and the healing of the paralysed man in Mark 2) but Job's experience gives the lie to those who automatically point the finger when someone becomes ill.

Further, we should take courage from this account on behalf of those whose reaction to illness is depression. Job was not blameless. It is likely that his descent into despair was hastened by his impatience with his friends, his misreading of God and his self-righteousness (Job 27:1-6). Nonetheless, Job's grim experience of reactive depression is handled with sympathy and understanding in the narrative. His low self-esteem (Job 3:3,11,12), impaired concentration (Job often seems to miss the point in his friends' discourse), loss of appetite (Job 6:6,7) sleeplessness (Job 7:4), rumination on past sin (Job 13:26) and desire for death (Job 3:3) are some of the sensitively portrayed symptoms of his melancholy.

Space forbids a detailed examination of how it was that Job eventually emerged from depression but it is worth making certain points for our own situations under three main headings: *our need to complain; our need to listen;* and *our need to repent.*

1.   Our need to complain

In chapter five, we will explore more fully the place of 'complaint' as seen in the light of the psalms of lament. For the moment, let us observe that Job, devastated by a series of profound losses, needed to give voice to how he felt. It appears that to start with, amidst the probable numbness of the initial impact of loss of family, possessions and his own health, his response was not only uncomplaining but also worshipful. We read:

> He fell to the ground in worship and said: 'Naked I came from my mother's womb, and naked I shall depart. The Lord gave and the Lord has taken away; may the name of the Lord be praised' (Job 1:20,21).

We too, when illness strikes, may find the Lord's grace to

respond in praise. We are in his hands and we can trust his wise plans, whether life abounds with his gifts or is impoverished by deprivation.

However, as we read on in the story of Job, we meet quite a different chain of reactions. His loathsome affliction was taking its toll and his body and spirit seem crushed by his sickness. His well-meaning friends were dumbfounded by his bleak situation: 'They sat on the ground with him for seven days and seven nights. No-one said a word to him, because they saw how great his suffering was' (Job 2:13).

The silent 'being with' Job that Eliphaz, Bildad and Zophar entered upon was in the best tradition of identifying with the afflicted. It was their later, wordy recriminations that really tore him to shreds. However, from the word go Job's anguish was let loose in loud lament. He cried out: 'May the day of my birth perish, and the night it was said, "A boy is born!"' and later: 'Why is life given to a man whose way is hidden, whom God has hedged in?' (Job 3:3,23). He complained vehemently that his worst fears had come upon him, that he had lost his peace and that God had cornered him. As the endless interchange with his 'comforters' continued, he turned directly to God, saying, 'Surely, O God, you have worn me out, you have devastated my entire household' (Job 16:7).

Those of us who contract serious and prolonged illness do need, as numbness gives way to fear and anger, to be able to express to God our strong feelings. God knows our inner turmoil and knows too that we can only begin to be helped by being honest with him.

2. Our need to listen

It has often been remarked that God has given us two ears but only one mouth. There is a place for telling God our complaint as we face affliction but we then have an even greater need to listen to his reply.

It took Job and his companions thirty-five long chapters of debate before they ran out of words! Even then it seemed to take an earth-shattering storm to still them. Job, within the earnest interchange with his would-be advisors, had also been crying to God – and now the Lord answers him out of the lightning and thunder. God's response to Job is devastating. The Lord of all declares his creative power, his control of the elements, his knowledge of everything he has made, his wisdom and providential care over the animal kingdom (Job 38–39). In a second phase of awesome revelation, God challenges Job with the words, 'Would you discredit my justice? Would you condemn me to justify yourself?' (Job 40:8).

We may not experience a confrontation as overwhelming as Job did but we do need to listen to God when we fall ill. Joy and I, sitting in the car on Colonsay, found the shift from lament to listening began to open us to God's peace once more. At such times, each of us should ask: What is it you want to show me, Lord, through this suffering? About yourself? About those around me? About myself? Many of us seem to require a period of serious sickness to stop us in our tracks and give us the space to reappraise life and its lessons. C. S. Lewis reminds us of the priceless opportunity to hear God amidst our afflictions:

> God whispers to us in our pleasure, speaks in our conscience, but shouts in our pains: it is His megaphone to rouse a deaf world.'[8]

3. Our need to repent

Job had ranted and raved against God within the darkness of his disease and depression. God allowed him ample time to have his say before silencing him with the terror and majesty of his shrouded presence. Job is driven to his knees, owning up to the emptiness of his words and the limitations of his knowledge. His meeting with the Holy One brings him to a deep penitence. He puts his godly sorrow into words: 'My ears had heard of you but now my eyes have seen you. Therefore I despise myself and repent in dust and ashes' (Job 42: 5,6).

At last the suffering Job has it right. He is a sinner, crumpled before a righteous and all-powerful God. And yet, this God is also compassionate. Job, in one of his anguished musings, had earlier groped towards the notion of a God who also loves when he uttered these wistful words: 'If only there were someone to arbitrate between us, to lay his hand upon us both, someone to remove God's rod from me, so that his terror would frighten me no more' (Job 9: 33,34). Somehow, in Job's repentance, this arbitrator was able to lay his hand on both the sufferer and Job's wrathful but loving God. This 'go-between' was the one of whom Job said, 'I know that my Redeemer lives, and that in the end he will stand upon the earth' (Job 19:25).

Job bows before God's sovereignty, discovers his forgiveness and thus finds restoration in all aspects of his life. Once again he is referred to by the Lord as 'my servant Job' (Job 1:8;42:8). Part of that service is to pray for his friends, who are guilty of not speaking 'what is right' of God. The revitalised Job reaches out in prayerful love and so experiences both the solace of the remaining members of his family and the Lord's abundant blessing. The dark valley of illness and depression is left behind; the years of prosperity stretch ahead – until Job died, 'old and full of years'.

Here is one of the deepest lessons for us as we engage with long-standing sickness. We need to complain, we need to listen and we need to repent. As we wait on God, we can begin to see where our anger has been sidetracked into wounded pride, our concern has degenerated into a faithless anxiety and our depression is tinged with self-pity. It is here that we should be reminded of the one who can 'lay his hand upon us both'. Joy and I on our Hebridean island knew afresh the restorative power of Jesus, the Lord who had died and risen again in order to bridge the rift between the afflicted – both carers and cared for – and their holy God.

In this healing of our relationship with God we may or may not experience Job's physical healing. In the next chapter we will consider the dilemma of why some are lifted out of their sickness and some are not.

3

YOU MUST SEEK HEALING!

Now I see that we can't demand or command that God do anything

Francis MacNutt

Life seemed very good for Nick. At the age of thirty he was at his peak: reasonably fit, enjoying cricket and sprint sports; working as a teacher at a well known boys' school; gifted musically and valuing good relationships with friends and family. It was April 1982 and he was driving south from a weekend with his parents – back to his flat in a West Country town, to his fellow-Christians in the local church and to his girlfriend, Karen.

Life was very good. Or was it? There was something on his mind which distracted him from the pleasant prospects ahead. Noticing a tight collar over the previous day or two, he had wondered whether he was putting on weight. However, now, while cruising along the motorway, he found himself fingering a decided lump on the side of his neck. There was no mistaking the swelling: firm, even hard, elongated like a bullet. He must see the doctor about it.

The days slipped by: the teaching job was as demanding as ever and Karen as pleasantly preoccupying as ever. The antibiotics he had been given for his neck 'gland' did not seem to have helped and a nagging backache took him for another medical opinion. He was promptly referred to a specialist who, ten days after removing a fragment of tissue for examination, told him that he had cancer. Nick was assured that it was a type of growth that could be treated and remembers his 'matter of fact' response and quiet resolve: 'I'm going to fight this.'

That night, as he followed his study of the Book of Judges, he found himself reading the story of Gideon in chapter six. In this account the Lord reasons with the reluctant leader of Israel, promising him victory over the Midianites. Gideon's final assurance from God came in words that demanded Nick's whole attention: '. . . the Lord said to him, "Peace! Do not be afraid. You are not going to die."' It is small wonder that this promise, originally given to an Israelite warrior, became Nick's treasured possession: he felt that God had spoken to him – very specifically: 'You, Nick, are not going to die of this cancer.' Five years later, he still holds the same conviction. How has his experience during the intervening time related to his belief in God's healing hand?

Over the next two years Nick and Karen had plenty of cause to doubt the apparently God-given certainty that came out of reading Judges 6:23. Nick, holding his convictions that he would not die of his illness, nonetheless faced investigations and treatment which must, at times, have made death an attractive option. The first of these trials came in the form of a lymphogram, in which a blue dye was pumped between his toes into the body's lymph system. His nagging back pain was made no easier by the metal table he had to lie on throughout the three hour infusion.

As is often the case in adversity, a sense of humour offset the unpleasantness of the procedure. Nick had been warned that parts of his body would look blue over the next twenty-four hours. A junior nurse looked wide-eyed when she saw the aristocratic colour of his urine. 'What's wrong?' Nick asked her. 'Look at the colour of your urine. It's blue!' she exclaimed. Her perplexity was not helped by his serious-faced response: 'Isn't everybody's? You know, I've been living under a misapprehension all my life!'

The result of the 'blue dye' test was not good. He was told

that his groin and neck were 'full of cancer growth' and that he would require four treatments of chemotherapy to combat the disease. Although he was able to keep on working during much of this period, his first two episodes of chemical treatment were followed by a week or more of vomiting and the progressive loss of all his body hair over a fortnight or so. He was determined to continue teaching and thought to hide his baldness with a wig. This ploy was a limited success since one sixth-former, mistaking his teacher's appearance for a half-hearted attempt at achieving a 'skin-head', commented, 'Cor! You've had a funny haircut!'

The climax of Nick's affliction came after his third treatment. Following the usual recovery pattern initially, he became dramatically worse after ten days when seized by episodes of sudden vomiting. His temperature had risen and he was admitted to hospital with an overwhelming infection of the bloodstream. There were serious doubts as to whether he would live through the night. His house doctor, knowing of Nick's and Karen's faith, shared her concern for his survival by saying to Karen, 'Pray that I'll choose the right antibiotic...' Karen prayed; the doctor chose – and, twenty-four hours later, the fever abated.

It is not hard to imagine Nick's reaction when, soon after this potentially fatal complication, his consultant raised the matter of the fourth, and final, dose of chemotherapy. Nick pleaded for a week's reprieve before submitting to the rigours of this necessary treatment. He remembers saying to the staff, 'This is the last time you'll do this to me' and to the specialist, at the end of the series, 'That's it now! No more chemotherapy.' The reply was that of a cautious professional and did not fill Nick with delight: 'We-e-ell, we'll see... In seven weeks' time we'll do a 'body scan'. There may still need to be more treatment – though of a different kind.'

Throughout the next seven weeks Nick – completely bald and weighing two stone less than he did before the illness – prayed nightly, 'Please God, no more treatment.' His heartfelt prayer was answered in that the body scan was reassuring. His consultant commented, 'I don't think we'll have to do any more at the moment. Some of the lymph nodes in the back are still too big. We'll keep an eye on them and if they go down, that's fine.' The implication, 'And if they don't go down, that's not so fine,' was not lost on the patient.

Amazingly, Nick, in spite of the gravity of his illness and the bombardment his body had received at the hands of medical science, had only two days off teaching during the coming school year. It was in the following summer that a further body scan revealed that he was not yet through his ordeal. He was told that the glands in his back, though no bigger, were still suspiciously large and that they should therefore be removed. Nick, under the impression that the procedure would be relatively minor, was dismayed when a well-intentioned anaesthetist calmly said to him just before the operation, 'You're the big one!'

He was, in fact, not only the 'big one' on that particular day's operating list but he was the 'big one' in terms of God's grace and bounty. The pathology lab. report on the removed glands announced that they were 'just dead tissue' and, during the coming months and years, Nick experienced not only the re-growth of his hair but a reasonable recovery of weight and vigour.

I have given a straight, factual account of a momentous eighteen months in Nick's life. It is important too that, as we seek to trace God's hand of healing on him, we also pick up with Karen's side of the story. A graduate from a northern university who also taught, she had known him for about three years at the time the cancer was found.

Her own private ordeal began when she was told early on that Nick stood a three per cent chance of getting through his illness and, 'If he gets through, he won't be the same person.' This medical opinion stressed Nick's vulnerability to infections, indicating a prospect of physical weakness and susceptibility. Worse was to follow for Karen when she learned that the man she cared for and hoped one day to marry would, because of the particular nature of his cancer and its treatment, lose his desire for love-making and would be sterile.

Amidst these long-term uncertainties were the pressing demands of the immediate. When Nick was admitted to hospital with septicaemia (following his third course of chemotherapy) she faced the probability of his imminent death. Somehow God's promise to Gideon – and so to Nick – must have looked very thin. Having seen him in an oxygen tent that evening, she was advised that he might be dead by the morning. She went home to her flat to wrestle with the bleak prospect and phoned a long-standing friend to tell him the news. He said, 'You pray all night; and I'll pray all night too.' She felt she could not pray for Nick's healing at this eleventh hour but realised she could, and would, ask God for peace for her loved one – whatever the night might bring. When she visited Nick at 6.30 a.m. the next day she found him lying calmly, his fever abated. His first comments to her that morning were of the deep sense of peace and of God's care towards him that he had experienced over the previous few days – 'like a child bathed in the Father's love.'

Meantime, Karen, like Mary before her, wondered at God's hand upon them and 'kept all these things in her heart'. However, this period of encouragement could not keep back her foreboding for long. Within three or four months she needed to visit her GP, requesting the 'hardest Valium you can give me'. He declined to give her Valium but over the next few weeks gave her hours of his time, which, in terms of her fears and worries, helped tide her over into the following year.

Paradoxically, it was soon after the hospital's declaration that Nick's glands, removed at the 'big' operation, were 'just dead tissue' that Karen's questions began to tumble one over the other. She wanted to marry Nick and, in time, have children by him. She plied the medical staff with her queries: 'Does the operation just show a remission? Or is it a cure? In effect, will he die or live during the next year? And if he is to live, and we marry, what of our sex life? What about children?' As a Christian, she did not find much support from the advice of one of the doctors, 'Why don't you and Nick shack up together and see if you like his sexuality?'

She sought hard facts from the hospital staff and she sought solace from God, 'Why, Lord, was it me that had to fall in love with someone who is sterile?' There was no comfort for Karen because there was no answer to one of life's unanswerable questions – and yet the question needed to be asked.

A decision had to be made. Nick and Karen loved each other, the medical outlook was cautiously hopeful and so, after months of agonising, an engagement ring was bought, 'knowing we wouldn't have children'. After a year of marriage without birth control, and within which Nick's ability to make love was found to be unimpaired, Karen conceived. And now, wonder of wonders, she and Nick have God's gift of a son – born, against the odds, of parents whose union was threatened by the shadow of death and, if that outlook proved mistaken, the prospect of infertility.

Like Nick and Karen, Patrick has experienced God's healing hand in the face of seemingly terminal illness. He was in his mid-sixties – at the point of retirement – when his voice first became croaky and he started to find swallowing difficult. However, it was over three years later that a 'quite deep-set' cancer of the larynx was diagnosed. After many years of doubt and debate with Christian friends, he had recently committed his life to Christ for the first time. The turning point had come in a village church in the Austrian Tyrol when Patrick, acutely aware of the presence of God, turned to his companion and said, 'I think it's time to stop talking... Let's kneel down and say a prayer.' His friend, a man of long-standing faith, replied, 'You really have got to make up your mind, haven't you?' Patrick, reflecting on his story some years later, added, 'It all became emphatic, inescapable...' And now, following his new beginning in Christ, something else had become 'emphatic' and 'in-escapable' – the hard-edged reality of cancer.

Patrick discovered the profoundest support in the church he attended. His vicar, soon after the possibility of cancer was raised, said to him, 'How wonderful you can now pray to a real, living Jesus. We shall all pray about it.' The house group he belonged to proved a tower of strength in support of this single, elderly man. This sense of solidarity with God's people and his Redeemer sustained him throughout the six weeks of daily radiotherapy. In spite of the tiring effect of the treatment he would walk the one and a half miles each way, finding renewed vigour from reading psalms as he sat, day by day, in the hospital waiting room.

Patrick looks back at the love and encouragement of his fellow-Christians and at the specialist's recent comment, 'I really think it's all healed' with gratitude, seeing his experience as a period of 'physical strengthening and spiritual growth'. As a 'thank you' to God he has committed himself to others in the church and community, and it is a rare Sunday that his bachelor home does not welcome five or six people to tea.

Nick, Karen and Patrick have all known something of God's healing power in the face of potentially fatal illness. And yet, as we are seeing throughout this book, theirs is not everyone's experience. Some do find renewed health and energy, even against the medical odds, many do not. Why is it that some – praying, faithful Christians – find at least a measure of healing of their afflictions, while others – also praying, faithful Christians – find no such respite? Is there a simple equation in which so many 'person-hours' of prayer (ten people praying for one hour being more effective than one for five minutes) plus certain degrees of faith equals so many units of healing? Some seem to argue that way, pointing an accusing finger at those 'fainthearts' whose illness continues on its restrictive and destructive path. Can they be right? And if they are, where is God in the equation? Do we have the sort of God who, if we say, 'Jump!' jumps? the sort of God that, if we get our 'prayer-faith' formula right, *automatically* heals?

Henry Frost, in his *Miraculous Healing,* tackles this dilemma head-on. In the opening chapters he gives detailed accounts of five people who were healed miraculously and then tells the stories of five others with medical histories and context of prayer and expectant faith that match the first group – who were not healed. The rest of the book explores the mystery of why some find physical wholeness and others do not and arrives at the statement that:

> Christ will choose health, strength and length of days for some of His saints; He will choose opposite experiences for the same saint at different times.[1]

This emphasis that the Lord makes choices about our health and sickness is, understandably, an unpopular one amongst many Christians today. At face value this view can conjure up a picture of the Almighty spinning a coin over the fate of each individual: 'Heads, I'll keep her fit and healthy; tails, she's in for trouble.' Such a picture of a deity who makes arbitrary decisions, parcelling out illnesses as if he had to dispense so many cancers, so many heart attacks by a certain deadline, is not only crude and repellent but is a far cry from the portrait of the one who is 'a compassionate and gracious God, slow to anger, abounding in love and faithfulness' (Ps 86:15). Let us, then, take a fresh look at certain aspects of healing in the Bible to see whether we can understand more fully why some, in crying to God, find health and others do not.

God is Healer

The Scriptures are quite clear that the Lord God is one who can and does bring healing to the needy. Following three days' march in the desert and the sweetening of the bitter waters of Marah, the revived Israelites hear the divine words: 'I am the Lord who heals you' (Ex 15:26). David praises the God who 'forgives all my sins and heals all my diseases' (Ps 103:3). In Isaiah the contrite are promised restoration: '"Peace, peace, to those far and near," says the Lord. "And I will heal them"' (Isa 57:19).

In the New Testament, the impact that Jesus, as God's all-powerful Son, made on the sicknesses of those he met is phenomenal. Morton Kelsey points out that nearly one-fifth

of the Gospel account is taken up with Christ's healings and
the debates that arose from them.[2] God's power to heal was
manifest through Jesus in a thoroughgoing way. Not only did
he heal those who suffered from so-called incurable
conditions – the deaf, dumb, blind, paralysed, deformed and
insane – but his healings were immediate, complete and,
apparently, lasting.[3] We pick up the flavour of the radical
nature of his touch in the story of the woman who had
endured heavy vaginal bleeding over twelve years. Her
expectant trust was fully rewarded:

> Jesus turned and saw her, 'Take heart, daughter,' he said,
> 'your faith has healed you.' And the woman was healed
> from that moment (Mt 9:22).

Further, both biblical insight and human experience reveal
that God heals by many means and in many ways.

God heals by many means

As we have seen, God can heal in spectacular fashion in a
manner we call miraculous. The origins of the meaning of the
word 'miracle' include both the wonderment at the
unusualness of an event and the significance of that event.[4]
Put these two ideas together and we have a 'miraculous sign' –
as in the turning of water into wine, which must have
dumbfounded the onlookers besides 'revealing Jesus's glory'
(see Jn 2:11). Henry Frost indicates this double aspect of
divine miracle when he writes:

> A miracle is supernatural; but it is not unnatural. A
> miracle is above law; but it is not opposed to law. A
> miracle is God working on a plane familiar to Himself, but
> unfamiliar to men, which, transcending human thought
> and explanation, becomes to men a wonder, marvel and
> sign.[5]

In the realm of healing, God can so speed up the body's
natural restorative functions or reverse an illness's destructive

sequence that the immediacy and completeness of the change is dubbed a miracle. Those around are filled with amazement and the event speaks to others of God's victory over disease.

However, God's healing powers are not limited to the dramatic quality of the miracle. By definition, a miracle is an exception to the rule. If miracles as 'temporary suspensions of natural laws' become commonplace and routine, they are no longer miracles. And yet God does heal in the everyday – by both natural and medical means.

God as Creator has given all life a prodigious capacity for repair and restoration. The recovery from a cut finger, a sprained ankle or a dose of flu is the outcome of remarkably complex processes within the body's cells and fluids. We tend to take it for granted that we get over such conditions and that God has made us so that, to take these three examples, we do not bleed to death, have a permanent limp nor automatically die from influenza.

As a doctor, I wish that the words of Ben Sira recorded in Ecclesiasticus 38:1–15 were part of the canon of Scripture! He writes: 'Honour the doctor with the honour that is his due in return for his services; for he too has been created by the Lord ... My son, when you are ill, do not be depressed, but pray to the Lord and he will heal you ... Then let the doctor take over – the Lord created him too – and do not let him leave you, for you need him.' In reality, there is comparatively little in the Bible about the arts of the physician, although we do have a number of pointers to God's use of various means as part of the healing process. Elijah's prostration over the widow's son may have been a form of artificial respiration (1 Ki 17:21); Isaiah requested 'a poultice of figs' for Hezekiah's boil (2 Ki 20:7); Jesus used both saliva by itself and to moisten clay in his encounters with the blind and mute (Mk 7:33;8:23; Jn 9:6,7); and James advocated anointing the sick with oil (Ja 5:14).

This range of 'ways and means', whatever their symbolism and medicinal purposes, remind us that the material world – animal, vegetable and mineral – is the Lord's and can be used to mediate healing. 'Everything God created is good, and nothing is to be rejected if it is received with thanksgiving' (1 Tim 4:4) could be the motto for every effort to tap natural resources for bringing relief and health to needy people. The age-old extraction of substances from medicinal herbs, the more modern synthesis of vital drugs, the use of X-rays and body scans in diagnosis, the harnessing of radiation to treat tumours, the development of increasingly sophisticated surgical techniques and the painstaking research behind all such medical advances can all be seen as good stewardship of what God the Healer has given.

Our danger is to praise the human body when natural healing takes place and to 'honour the doctor' when a medical cure is found, leaving any thanksgiving towards God strictly for the miraculous. Thus 'the Lord who heals' is pushed to the margin of our day by day experience, simply being brought in as a last resort to do something about the incurable and terminal.

God heals in many ways

There is a modern trend to see healing in terms of the whole person so that a quest for, say, physical health will take note of the need for wholeness in all other aspects of life: emotional, mental, spiritual, creative, social, and so on. Let us take the example of a man in his early forties with a duodenal ulcer. Any comprehensive approach to healing will not only give advice on diet, the restriction of alcohol, the avoidance of smoking and aspirin-like drugs but will also take into consideration any emotional strains within his marriage, mental stresses at work and inner conflicts he may have over spiritual or moral issues.

Although such 'holistic' approaches have a contemporary ring they simply mirror a fundamentally Judaeo-Christian view of our humanity – for 'the Hebrew did not see man as a combination of contrasted elements but as a unity that might be seen under a number of different aspects.'[6] Even though the Bible often talks of the 'heart', the 'flesh', the 'soul', the 'spirit' – as well as, more graphically, the 'bowels', the 'liver', the 'kidneys' – each area of the body or inner life basically emphasises this or that feature within overall human experience. God is concerned with the whole of life. We see something of his intent in the Old Testament word *shalom* (peace be with you), of which Morris Maddocks has written: 'it means well-being in the widest sense of the word – prosperity, bodily health, contentedness, good relations between nations and men, salvation.'[7]

In the New Testament, that all-embracing word 'salvation', as used by Maddocks, is often synonymous with the ideas of 'health' and 'wholeness'. For example, the Greek work *sozo* is frequently used with the sense of deliverance from evil in order to heal the entire person. We find this usage in the stories of Jairus's daughter and the woman with heavy bleeding (Mk 5:21–43), as well as in Christ's encounters with needy men and women in Gennesaret:

> And everywhere he went – into villages, towns or countryside – they placed the sick in the market-places. They begged him to let them touch even the edge of his cloak, and all who touched him were healed (made whole) (Mk 6:56).

Paul Tournier, in his book *Creative Suffering*, puts his finger on the all-inclusive nature of our Lord's healing: 'Doctors seek to heal the whole by healing the parts, whereas Jesus, it seems, healed the parts by healing the whole.'[8]

However, there is another side to the coin of God's dealings with human need. His concern reaches out not only to the whole of life but also to each and every aspect. In other words, God cares about the particular as well as the general. We see this in the way Jesus dealt with the specific nature of the afflictions people brought to him. He gave sight to the blind, mobility to the paralysed, deliverance to the demon-possessed, forgiveness to the guilty, inner peace to the anxious and a lightening of the load to the burdened. And so the Lord, who works to bring overall health, is also the Lord who meets us in the details of our suffering.

And yet, we cannot dictate to God the Healer either the manner or the method of our healing. As we have seen he heals by many means: natural, medical, miraculous. Both Nick and Patrick have experienced God's hand upon them through his wonder-giving interventions as well as in the quieter, everyday processes of professional care and the body's intrinsic powers of recovery. Moreover, God in his moves towards bringing wholeness into our lives often deals primarily with this or that aspect of our existence. His handling of our situation may or may not tally with what we seek of him. Many, for example, wanting the removal of some physical affliction, have met with a God who seems to respond little to their request but, in his wisdom, brings a deep inner peace instead. I am reminded here of Jacob who, as he wrestled with a stranger till daybreak, met with God. We read that this encounter led to blessing – and, as the sun rose on the scene, to a limp! (Ge 32:22–32). As we seek healing, God meets us and blesses us but often leaves us with the marks of our continuing frailty and need of him. To use Gerard Hughes' phrase, he is the 'God of surprises'.[9]

This brings us to consider that God is sovereign.

God is Sovereign

We have already noted that the idea of a God who chooses our encounters with illness and their outcomes is open to caricature. We rightly fear a picture of him as an arbitrary despot who can will sickness on one life and decide not to on another. What view do we see of God's sovereignty in the Bible?

First, we need to come to terms with the insight that God is not only Healer but, in some sense or other, he also 'sends' affliction and illness. In Exodus 15:26 the declaration that he is 'the Lord who heals' is set in the context that, in the past, he had brought diseases upon the Egyptians. This same daunting prospect is seen in Habakkuk 3:5 where the prophet says of the Lord, 'Plague went before him; pestilence followed his steps.'

Perhaps the clue to this dark enigma lies in the phrase used of God in the setting of the Passover when the 'angel of death' was to visit every household: 'He will not permit the destroyer to enter your house and strike you down' (Ex 12:23). We find a similar perspective in the harrowing story of Job when Satan is allowed by God to afflict Job 'with painful sores from the soles of his feet to the top of his head' (Job 2:7). The account suggests that it is the Adversary who brings calamity into people's lives as he goes 'roaming through the earth . . . to and fro' (Job 1:7). He is like a ferocious creature which is given a limited permission to cause suffering: he is leashed by a certain length of rope and can go so far but no further. The devil and his angels have a certain strength and influence in spreading havoc but their freedom is held in check by a greater will and power.

At first sight this scenario may bring us little comfort. All we know is that we suffer – and the debate, whether our sickness is sent by God, the devil or has come about through human folly, passes over our heads as we roll on our beds of pain. And yet, as we think further, there *is* solace in the knowledge that God is ultimately in charge – and that solace lies in the sort of God he is.

In everyday life where others are in charge of us (parents, instructors, employers, people in senior positions) we are most reassured if their intent towards us is caring, if they have a measure of know-how and if they have enough power to put their good will and wisdom into action. As an extension of the point, our encouragement at the hand of God upon us can be immeasurably greater.

We find, first, that his intentions for us are for our good. As he said to those in exile: 'I know the plans I have for you . . . plans to prosper you and not to harm you, plans to give you hope and a future' (Jer 29:11). We discover the same loving concern expressed throughout the New Testament – as in 2 Peter 3:9, where we read of God: 'He is patient with you, not wanting anyone to perish.' In the face of declining health, however we understand its origins, we should never doubt God's compassion and care.

Further, we find in him the perfect blend of wisdom (to know what is best) and power (to effect that best). Daniel worshipped the God who reveals mysteries in these words: 'Praise be to the name of God for ever and ever, wisdom and power are his' (Da 2:20). We see these same attributes in the Son, of whom it is written, 'to those whom God has called . . . Christ the power of God and the wisdom of God' (1 Co 1:24). Jim Packer writes of the comfort that is ours in these aspects of God's character:

> Wisdom without power would be pathetic, a broken reed; power without wisdom would be merely frightening; but in God boundless wisdom and endless power are united, and this makes him utterly worthy of our fullest trust.[10]

God is Father

It is because our sovereign God wishes well for us and has the wisdom and power to carry out his worthy plans that we can give him our 'fullest trust' – even in our pains and afflictions. It is because he is also our Father that we can cry out to him in our need.

Here, as always, Jesus is our example. In Gethsemane, facing an adversity whose awefulness both encompasses and goes beyond our worst experiences, he falls to the ground and prays: '*Abba*, Father, everything is possible for you. Take this cup from me. Yet not what I will, but what you will' (Mk 14:36). His relationship with the Father had always been open, trusting and dependent. Jesus had said to the Jews, 'I tell you the truth, the Son can do nothing by himself; he can do only what he sees his Father doing, because whatever the Father does the Son also does' (Jn 5:19). Further, he had gone on to say that that bond of filial submission is a bond of love, 'For the Father loves the Son' (verse 20). And so, ever obedient to the Father and secure in his love, Jesus cries,

'*Abba*, Father' as he confronts the mounting horror of the coming day.

The word *Abba* he uses is Aramaic and was one of the terms of everyday family life. Although many have translated it as 'Daddy', signifying a young child's word for father, there is some danger of over-familiarity in using the language of the nursery. In fact, it has been pointed out that *Abba* was a word used by grown-up sons and daughters even before Christ's time and that the best rendering is simply 'Dear Father'. As Professor C. F. D. Moule has written, '[Jesus] uses the Abba address to offer God his complete obedience. The intimate word conveys not a casual sort of familiarity but the deepest, most trustful reverence.'[11]

Our Lord's example and teaching on the Father give us a picture, then, of one who is loving and trustworthy. At times the image of God as 'Daddy' may be helpful in stressing our need for a childlike dependency. However, children can be precocious and cocky and we should avoid a portrayal of God that encourages presumption. Rather, he is to be the 'Dear Father' in a relationship that is close without being too familiar, calling for 'the deepest, most trustful reverence'.

Where does all this leave you and me in our desire for healing? I suggest that Jesus's prayer in the Garden is a model for us as we face affliction of any sort, including that of serious illness. Let us consider each phrase in turn.

Abba, Father

In the Sermon on the Mount, Jesus cites the parental affection of members of his audience as an indicator of the Father's concern and generosity. Having asked the rhetorical questions as to who would give his son a stone instead of bread or a snake instead of a fish, he says:

> If you, then, though you are evil, know how to give good gifts to your children, how much more will your Father in heaven give good gifts to those who ask him! (Mt 7:11).

The trouble is that some of us have had fathers who, we feel, might well have given us a stone instead of bread or a snake instead of a fish! We may look back at fathers whom we reckon we never really knew (Would they have given a fish or a snake? We are not quite sure) or we may have been on the receiving end of undoubted fatherly vindictiveness (there is no doubt; it would have been a snake and not a fish!). As I look through my files of people I have counselled over the years I find a high proportion of those in trouble either have fathers who are shadowy, ineffective figures or who have, in one way or another, undermined and belittled their children.

As we face serious forms of illness, then, many of us may have real difficulty in turning our fears into prayer to the Father. We have, perhaps, learnt not to expect much from our earthly fathers and that lack of trust can run very deep. Jesus's '*Abba*, Father' cry is an invitation for us to take the plunge. He has shown us what the Father is like and, even though our own fathers have fallen short, here is one who gives 'good gifts to those who ask him'. Maybe we need also to forgive our own fathers, to ask God's forgiveness for our resentments and seek his help to begin to understand and love those we feel have abused us.

We read that, as we open our lives to the Son, his Spirit enables us too to cry '*Abba*, Father' (Ro 8:15). Let us do just that in our hour of need.

Everything is possible for you

If we are to approach the Father in our pain and affliction we must try to see that everything is possible for him. God *is* Healer and his hands are not tired. He has no difficulty in diagnosing puzzling medical conditions, in altering the usual course of chronic illness or curing diseases that are normally deemed incurable. This is the God who created the wonders and glory of the universe out of nothing, who stills the storms, provides for the needy and, in his Son, turned water into wine, walked on water, healed countless people and, greatest of all, wrought salvation for fallen humanity. With God all things are possible. Kathryn Kuhlmann, in her book *I Believe in Miracles,* expresses the right expectancy when she writes, 'I am not a woman with great faith – I am a woman with a little faith in the Great God!'[12]

Take this cup from me

As we turn to the Father, remembering that nothing is too great for his accomplishment, we need to put our desires into words. Jesus did not beat about the bush. He was in the tightest of corners and his prayer was straight to the point: 'Take this cup from me.' He saw the reality of the coming hours as an outpouring of the bitter draught of God's judgment and asked the Father for its removal.

Our prayers, as we face illness, do need to be specific: 'Take *this* cup from me.' Nick, battling with cancer and in a particular state of exhaustion, asked God that there should be no more chemotherapy. Karen, at an earlier stage in Nick's disease, felt she could not pray for healing but could request a deep peace for her loved one.

This attitude of particularising – 'Please God, relieve the pain', 'Bring me safely through this operation, 'Halt the progress of this illness' – encourages the one who prays to see that the God of the impossible can meet any specific need. This concentration on bringing the details of our adversity to the Father is the exact opposite of the vague nature of many prayers where there is no real anticipation of an answer. Francis MacNutt's beatitude typifies the latter's lack of hope: 'Blessed are those who expect nothing, for they shall not be disappointed.'[13]

Yet not what I will, but what you will

Sadly, what is here an essential part of the Son's prayer to the Father is seen by many as a cop-out. They tell us, 'When you ask for healing, do not hedge your bets. Avoid phrases like "if it's your will"... realise it always *is* God's will to heal; claim that healing and thank him for it. If you don't appear to be any better, just ignore how you feel; remind yourself that you *are healed.*' This kind of view poses a dilemma for a lot of people who wonder how to pray for healing. If it is true that God *always* wills our health in this life, then there is strong logic in removing any 'ifs' and 'buts' from our praying. Just as we would not pray, 'God, forgive me – if it is your will' so to ask, 'Lord, heal me – if it is your will' would raise a false perspective that brings a quite unnecessary degree of uncertainty into the request.

But is it *always* God's will to heal our afflictions in the here and now? Our section on God's sovereignty suggests otherwise. Further, do we honour him by declaring that we are healed when all our senses speak to the contrary? Either we are healed or we are not, and, if all the evidence points to the latter, do we respect the Lord of the body by denying reality? What sort of crazy scene would it have been in the Gospel record if the blind man had groped his way unseeingly from Jesus and declared, 'Praise God! I am healed!'? This is not to deny that the Lord can heal gradually but, in such circumstances, an honest 'I believe God is healing me', or even 'I hope God is healing me', is far better than a make-believe 'God has healed me', spoken through teeth gritted against the discomforts of a disease's continuing presence.

There can, of course, be no doubt that God wills wholeness in every part of our being as our destiny in Christ – and we shall look at that more fully in the final chapter. And yet, the Bible also shows that God sometimes brings immediate healing, sometimes he restores after a period of delay and sometimes he allows adversity to continue, promising his enabling for the daily battle. Examples of the variety of God's will include: the dramatic healing of Naaman's 'leprosy' in which, once he obeyed Elisha's command, 'his flesh was restored and became clean like that of a young boy' (2 Ki 5:14); the eventual renewal of Job's health and fortune after a protracted time of suffering and uncertainty; and the Lord's response to Paul's three-fold prayer that his 'thorn in the flesh' be taken away: 'My grace is sufficient for you, for my power is made perfect in weakness' (2 Cor 12:9).

Just as some see the inclusion of an 'if it be your will' in a prayer for healing as an escape clause, so others (often, in fact, the same people!) object to allowing Paul's experience to be viewed as a pattern for coping with illness. Two main arguments are used against this conclusion: one is that the 'thorn in the flesh' probably referred to the apostle's opponents or to some particularly provoking fellow-Christian; the other is that Paul's 'visions and revelations from the Lord' (verse 1) were unique to him and, thereby, so were the 'thorn' and God's reply to his prayers. In my own experience of recurring blindness I have met both these lines of thought in debate with others – people who felt that the Pauline situation was a soft option for those who should be busy claiming God's healing.

In fact, there is uncertainty about what, or who, the 'thorn in the flesh' was. As Colin Brown indicates, the context of 2 Corinthians 11–12 suggests 'weakness or hardship' and is a 'celebration of triumph over disability and hardship'.[14] As has been pointed out elsewhere, the very lack of clarity about the 'thorn' is no accident because the nature of this passage establishes an important principle for all who face adversity: *that, at times, God chooses to say 'No' to our pleas for changed circumstances and declares to us 'My grace is sufficient for you.'* Whether Paul was battling with epilepsy, an eye ailment, a vicious enemy, an irritating fellow-believer or an inferiority complex is beside the point. The Holy Spirit, it seems, has kept the application general so that we are not trapped into seeing these words just for, say, epileptics or those goaded by other Christians (or, for that matter, only those with 'visions and revelations from the Lord').

In the face of illness, as with any other calamity that comes our way, it is right for us to turn to our Father. In echoing the words of Jesus's Gethsemane prayer we are reminded that God is Healer (for everything is possible for him) and is also sovereign (for his will must have the last word). It is essential that we allow God to be God in our lives – whether he brings complete or partial healing, the uncertainties of a delayed recovery or permits the affliction its natural course, offering his daily grace and sustenance. Nick and Patrick have both experienced substantial healing – though the one is less robust than he used to be and the other still finds his voice hoarse when he is tired. I, through God's use of medical and natural means, know a measure of restoration: I can now see well with one eye and a chronic infection is gradually clearing up after a troublesome seven years or so. Jonathan, whom we thought about in the first chapter and to whom we shall come back in chapter five, was not to recover. All four of us, in spite of our varying degrees of suffering, would lay claim to something of God's power being 'made perfect in weakness'. John Wimber has the perspective right when he says of God:

> His sovereignty, lordship and kingdom are what bring healing. Our part is to pray 'Thy kingdom come' – and trust him for whatever healing comes from his gracious hand. And if in this age it does not come, then we have assurance from the atonement that it will come in the age to come.[15]

OLD ALREADY

Weakness and pain helped me to study how to die;
that set me studying how to live

Richard Baxter

Duchenne muscular dystrophy is fortunately a rare medical condition. Only about thirty in a million are likely to suffer from the affliction and twenty-nine of these will almost certainly be male. Anna is one of the very few women who battles with this particular muscle disorder.

Anna, now in her late twenties, is the only daughter born to Guy and Rosemary Harris. She and her three brothers grew up in a caring household where Christ was honoured and the rich variety of the created order appreciated. The worlds of literature, drama, music, painting and fashion were all seen as legitimate areas for Christ-centred exploration. Life for the Harrises, in spite of the usual strains and tensions that beset families, promised well: they were gifted, intelligent, reasonably well off, outgoing and godly. And yet one particular concern would not go away. Anna, though a lively and bright child, was late in standing and walking, seemed reluctant to run and fell over more readily than her brothers had at a similar age. When she was two the doctors diagnosed Duchenne muscular dystrophy, informing her parents that she would become confined to a wheelchair by the age of ten and would probably die before her teen years were over.

Anna, at least in some respects, was to prove medical opinion wrong. As she looks back she cannot recall, understandably, a time when her limbs would do all she wanted them to. However, she was determined to do her best to keep up with other children. Although she says that the muscular dystrophy was always 'so much *me*', her extraverted spirit kept her on the move. Even so one of her main frustrations in the earlier years was that, if she fell over, she would flounder, unable to get up unaided. Despite her perseverance, walking gradually became more difficult so that by the age of fourteen she could hardly put one foot in front of the other. Defeat would still not be tolerated and her friends at the girls' school would make sure she moved from one class to another at their speed. Anna, though normal in other respects, is short-limbed and has very thin arms. Her weight now is only four stone, and so, in her mid-teens, she was a light burden to her eager friends. The mode of transport was varied and effective: sometimes she was carried by two girls as she sat on a chair; at other times she was borne aloft, piggyback style; and, for a change, she was on occasions transported in a friend's arms, cradled like a baby.

By the time she began to attend the local university to study Classics, Anna was spending much of her waking life in a wheelchair. Most of her schoolfriends had left the area and it was not easy, at first, to establish new friendships. In time though, several students became very special to her, and Anna, within the restrictions of her physical frame, was able to enjoy both the academic and social aspects of university life.

It was after graduation that the 'real dip' came. Her new friends had dispersed to find jobs and she, unemployed, was left at home with her parents. There were frustrations on both sides. Anna, unable now to stand up without help, was extremely dependent on Guy and Rosemary and, after the excitements of student life, all on the domestic front seemed an anticlimax. Her mother and father, for their part, had the continuing tie of a daughter in her early twenties whose need for mobility pressed in on their own plans. Nonetheless, Anna had a steady determination to push out the frontiers and Guy and Rosemary maintained their very practical love for their gifted daughter.

Following a year of trying to sort out a possible career – taking lessons in drama, assisting in an amateur production of light opera, writing to the BBC, taking part in one or two radio programmes – Anna was able to take up a series of contracts in the world of disabled theatre. In time, she was able to move to London where she shares a flat with Marjorie, a caring Christian friend who related to Anna in a straightforward, unpatronising way.

Let us, in this chapter, look at the difficulties and potential triumphs in lives that have become 'old already', illustrating our points from Anna's story and the experiences of one or two others who have battled with serious handicap. If there is one word which sums up the feelings of the physically deprived that word is *frustration*. We will consider that frustration in two main areas: a *loss of independence* and a *loss of spontaneity*.

Loss of Independence

In chapter one we discussed how dependency is one of the things we greatly fear as we face acute illness 'out of the blue'. Where, as in Anna's case, there is a progressive loss of physical function that fear becomes a reality. When mobility, sight, hearing, speech or memory deteriorate or vanish, then the frustration at a loss of independence can be devastating for both patient and loved ones.

It was only a month or so before her marriage to Clive that Sarah became ill. The symptoms were vague – a feeling of sickness and extreme tiredness – and the situation did not seem serious. However, the unwellness persisted and dulled the edge of excitement over the wedding. Medical opinion muttered something about a 'virus', though Sarah wondered whether the doctors were putting it all down to 'pre-marriage nerves'. When her general malaise gave way to numbness in her hands and a tendency to stumble, Sarah began to suspect multiple sclerosis (MS) – a condition she had met many times in her work as a nurse. Her suspicions were soon confirmed.

This was a depressing diagnosis to receive because the one predictable thing about MS is its unpredictability! On the other hand it is a malady that some patients survive with little disability over a stretch of up to fifty years. Sarah, however, had experienced a gradual deterioration over the first few years of her illness. Within that time she and Clive have had the joy of bringing their own baby, Matthew, into the world. This little one, seen very much as God's gracious gift, has, nonetheless, emphasised the frustration of Sarah's loss of independence. When asked what were the worst aspects of her situation, she listed her inability to write, drink without a straw, cook and do the housework, adding that she could not even hold Matthew while she stood or tried to walk. She concluded, 'I don't feel I can function as a housewife or mother.' Sarah's pain is compounded by Clive's anguish as he does his best for his wife and child.

A loss of independence can be catastrophic for all involved whatever the age of the sufferer: Anna was only fourteen when she had to trust her body to her schoolfriends; Sarah was in the prime of her life when MS was diagnosed; and, to take a contrast, my father, Fred, was in his late seventies when he was felled by a severe stroke.

Fred had been a man of exceptional bounce and vigour. He had always been a practical person and his retirement from the GPO released his energies for a host of neighbourly jobs for both the local church and the wider community. A few years before his death, my parents moved to live near our family and Fred became quite a landmark in the nearby High Street – up and down which he would cycle, displaying brown, muscular legs in the summer and sporting one or other of a series of distinctive hats in the winter.

It was Christmas 1983 when the first telltale signs of a virulent form of bladder cancer began to show. Blood in his urine led, via a string of hospital investigations, to increasing lower abdominal pain and a course of radiotherapy. While waiting for the seventh of a series of twenty-five treatments he collapsed in the Out-Patients. As he came round in a hospital bed he woke to a complete paralysis of his right side and the loss of any power of coherent speech. My mother and I still vividly remember the look of bewilderment on his distorted face as his eyes, seeking ours, asked, 'What does it all mean?'

It goes without saying that the following weeks were times of great distress for all who knew Fred, or Gramp as he was fondly called by his seven grandchildren. His loss of independence was complete, all his efforts to respond to physiotherapy, occupational and speech therapy making no impression on the density of the stroke. Meanwhile, the cancer gnawed away in his pelvic region. When not too distracted by pain or puzzlement, his old humour would try to rise up through his clouded mind: a glimmer of a twinkle in his eyes; a lopsided grin or a shrug of his left shoulder would be indicators of some half-formed joke. Although the articulation of words had gone, a rudimentary sense of music remained and he would attempt the tunes of his London childhood through a sequence of mouthed popping sounds. His frustration at absolute dependency gave way, in time, to resignation and a peaceful death. His was a Lenten dying: he was struck down on Shrove Tuesday and was buried following a service of godly sorrow on Maundy Thursday.

Loss of Spontaneity

George Orwell in *Animal Farm*, writes of the farm animals' leader, a fierce looking pig called Napoleon: '[He] has commanded that once a week there should be held something called a Spontaneous Demonstration.'[1] For many of us genuine moments of spontaneity are rare: at best our sense of immediacy is, like Napoleon's 'demonstration', a somewhat contrived affair. However, those who are reasonably healthy do at least have opportunities for leaping in the air, embracing a neighbour or dancing the night away. Many who are physically handicapped have severe limitations on such self-expression. They know the frustration of a loss of spontaneity.

This impairment was obvious in Sarah's crushing acknowledgment that she could not even hold her own baby while standing or walking. Her weak limbs and poor balance made this impossible. And so, as Matthew grew, Sarah could no longer respond spontaneously if they were alone in the house together. Any caring woman (and many caring men) can imagine something of the distress Sarah feels as she longs to pick up and cradle her fretful infant in her arms.

Anna, too, suffers a loss of immediacy in the day by day handling of her life. She describes herself as a 'very spontaneous person' and I am sure, with an averagely strong young woman's body, she would be one of those who would, given half the chance, leap in the air, embrace a neighbour or dance the night away. Instead, she has to stifle her impulses in a way that goes against the grain of her outgoing personality. Sometimes she is thus held back from affectionate physical contact with a close friend. At other times her more negative emotions are complicated by her immobility.

For example, she often needs the practical help of a taxi-driver to pick her up, literally, from her London flat, drive her to her destination and then manhandle her to her rendezvous. Every so often she finds herself at the mercy of a driver who adopts a patronising or sarcastic manner. In such an instance, Anna feels trapped. She relies on the driver for physical handling and transport, and in this procedure she needs to relate to him in order to deal with direction-giving and payment. When she is irritated by his demeaning attitude she feels she can only deal with the situation by silence. Her frail body prevents her from the spontaneity of getting up and walking away from condescending behaviour. It is not that she *would*, necessarily, stride away in similar circumstances if her frame were healthy, so much as that she has no choice in the matter.

There are many aspects to this twin loss of independence and spontaneity. For example, there is a paradox in that the former loss often involves too much physical contact and the latter too little. In a loss of independence the proximity of those who do practical things, particularly if there is fuss or

condescension, can be intolerable. In a loss of spontaneity the
sufferer may find it impossible to rise to the occasion where
the longed-for closeness seems available. The moment of
reassuring intimacy may come and go before a semi-
paralysed limb can be mobilised or a speechless grunt with
the right inflexion made. In a loss of independence the
disabled may feel, 'I can't do what I want;' and in a loss of
spontaneity, 'I can't be what I want.'

Before we look more positively at coping with physical
handicap let us underline the frustrations of being 'old
already' through Anna's poem of that title:

> She is old young
> it's not a question of becoming
> she is
>
> Another morning
> another day challenges her awake
> a day takes on the importance of a year
> when you feel near
> the last lap
> the first job is to unlock those alien joints
> her heart and mind leap beyond her ability
> weighed down not by blankets but an intangible power shortage
> stick arms that won't fill out
> all her body in refugee proportions
> sits slumped lies back bent twisted
> feet that couldn't support a flea
>
> She drops into bed and battles with her clothes
> while trampish thoughts
> suggest a fully-clothed night
> an old lady's hand stretching feebly for the light
> knocks it down
> a young girl's mind despises the pathetic scene
> which should be a mere lightning flash of her day
> strength leaks out of her bag-bone body
> imperceptibly
> like the tiniest hole in a tyre
> harmless at first
> finally devastating[2]

Coping with Handicap

Already, in writing about Anna, Sarah and Fred, we have
picked up hints for coping with serious physical disability.
Each of these people has found ways of surviving the
frustrations of a loss of independence and spontaneity. And
yet there is more to dealing with being 'old already' than
simple survival. Let us see that there are many means of grace
which can lead to a fulness of life, even against the odds. I do
not say this lightly for I am aware that for many there seems
to be no hope along the path of handicap. Nonetheless, there
are people and perspectives that can, like Hopeful and his
encouragement of Christian in *The Pilgrim's Progress*, lift up
the downcast at their point of greatest need. Let us consider
the healing properties of *other people, creativity* and a *sense
of humour* before looking more directly at *God and
weakness*.

1. Other people

Jean-Paul Sartre, from the viewpoint of his atheistic
existentialism, declared, 'Hell is other people.' We can
proclaim that, rightly understood 'The path to heaven is
other people.' There is a new and God-centred principle of life
(the 'law of Christ' that brings freedom) which is fulfilled as
we respond to and receive from other people.[3] The Pauline
injunction to, 'Carry each other's burdens' (Gal 6:2) is never
more searching and demanding than when we seek to obey it
in the context of physical handicap. We can think about what
this means, firstly, for family and secondly, for friends.

(a) Family

A Chinese proverb declares that, 'Nobody's family can hang
out the sign "Nothing the matter here"' and when physical
disability strikes one member of a family there is a great deal
'the matter' for all others. And it is this shared affliction
which is both pain and opportunity for those involved.

Anna's mother, Rosemary, in writing of how she had felt when the diagnosis of muscular dystrophy was first made, admitted her 'numbness, followed by weeping and excessive irritability'. Such a grief reaction was necessary before she was able to proclaim, 'But beyond that we had a deep feeling of trusting God in this situation for Anna, for our other children and for ourselves.' This confidence in a God who provides has coloured the detailed daily caring that Guy and Rosemary have given to their daughter throughout the twenty-five years or so of her affliction.

Within families, there will often be a degree of mutuality in the caring. The more love is shown by the carers the more the sufferer responds with affection. Everyone gives; everyone receives. Sometimes there is a marked balance of compassion – not least where two people who love each other share a common affliction. This is true for Reg and Linda Foster.

Reg and Linda were born with cerebral palsy, a condition which affects posture, movement and muscle tone. Special schooling was needed and both, suffering from complete paralysis of the legs, are confined to wheelchairs. They met at a residential home for the handicapped, fell in love and got engaged. There was much resistance from the authorities to them marrying and the engagement period became very drawn out. However, Reg and Linda persisted in their commitment and have now, in their mid-forties, been married ten years or so.

Living together in a flat, they receive good support from the district nurses and a rota of Christians from the local church. Reg, in spite of his immovable legs and grossly deformed spine, has strong arms and somehow manoeuvres himself to do most of the housework, including making the bed and cooking the meals. Their life together is lived at the slowest of paces. At weekends (when the nurses do not need to visit, in order to hurry up the process for the Fosters to attend the Day Centre), the sequence of getting up, washing and dressing can take two hours or so. Despite their lifelong frustrations, there is a great deal of tenderness between Reg and Linda. The support they give each other is symbolised in the care they both take in remembering their wedding anniversary. The wonder that two severely disabled people should discover the joys and trials of marriage together is hinted at in a recent comment by Reg: 'I never thought I would get married – but, here we are!'

(b) Friends

In chapter one we saw the importance of support from others to those who are afflicted 'out of the blue'. When someone is struck down with physical disability a caring family has no option but, after the initial shock, to at least try to rise to the occasion. In friendship there is more choice. A friend can stand back for a while and weigh things up from a distance, before deciding to offer assistance or continue in the background. A caring friend will learn to gauge this right, asking, 'Is it best for me to stay available and wait to be asked for help?' or, 'Is it now the time to try to engage with the situation?' Sometimes a family, distressed at the sufferings of a loved one, desperately wants to be left alone. At other times there is a deep longing for someone from outside who will step in and shoulder some of the burden.

Friendship can have the advantage of a greater objectivity. A family can be quite blinkered about its members: because they have lived together for so long each can hold somewhat prejudiced views about the others. For example, the foibles and excesses of teenage children can be held over by parents in a way that prevents them from seeing a maturing process under their very noses. Conversely, the younger members of a family can retain earlier memories of their parents which make it difficult for them to accept that mother and father can actually change their views or ways of behaving. Perhaps this is why the Book of Proverbs sometimes elevates friendship above family: 'A friend loves at all times, and a brother is born for adversity' (Pr 17:17) and 'A man of many companions may come to ruin, but there is a friend who sticks closer than a brother' (Pr 18:24). Here we see that there are 'friends' and 'friends': it is one thing to know a lot of people but the hallmarks of true friendship are closeness and a caring consistency.

Julie Donnelly had something of that experience in her relationship with Elaine Brook.[4] Julie, in her mid-thirties, works as a switchboard operator in London and has been blind since the age of eight. In the earlier years of adulthood she suffered a great deal of tension and anxiety about venturing out with a white stick, into what felt like a hostile world. Eventually she was able to own Bruno, a yellow Labrador guide dog whose company gave her confidence to live life as normally as possible. However, it was meeting Elaine that opened up Julie's horizons to adventure beyond the streets of London.

Elaine Brook had been a keen mountaineer from the age of nineteen. She graduated from British hills and the Alps to climbs in the Canadian Rockies, on Baffin Island in the Arctic and, in time, on Himalayan expeditions. Her friendship with Julie led (inevitably, given Julie's desire to push the frontiers) to climbing trips together. As in all good relationships there was a bond of mutuality. While Julie learned how to climb on Lakeland crags, Elaine discovered the untapped riches of her own non-visual senses – the feel, smells and sounds of a hillside adding to her appreciation of the wild places.

Through Elaine's friendship Julie caught the bug of mountaineering. One November in the early 1980s the two women set out on the three week trek to Everest Base Camp, from which they planned to climb the 18,000 foot peak of Kala Patthar. On the upper slopes of their successful ascent Julie was assailed by altitude sickness and dehydration. Elaine, in seeking to help her blind companion, not only revealed the consistency of her love and their closeness but also the strengthening quality of friendship that is both reassuring and bracing.[5] She records what she said to Julie:

> Okay, you can't see, but then I can't carry as much as a Sherpa. It's all relative. If we're proving anything at all it is that attitude and state of mind are what count. What

people seem to miss is that it's fun for me as well, because we're doing it together. It gives me a totally new perspective.

2. Creativity

Doris Lessing, the novelist, said in a radio interview in May 1980 that, 'Art is rooted in corruption, particularly in illness.' John Milton's blindness, descending on him in his mid-forties, and Beethoven's deafness, progressively debilitating from the age of thirty till his death at fifty-six, are well known examples of 'Art rooted in illness'. It is not, though, just amongst the giants of literature and music that we can see creativity born out of suffering.

We have already picked up something of the way Anna's medical condition has been the soil of some very fertile artistic endeavour. We are not arguing here that achievement in the Arts can only arise from affliction, so much as that the urge to create is often given wings by the need both to express and overcome frustration. Anna's acting, singing and writing of poetry can speak to us of the crushing nature of disability and the will to triumph.

Creativity is, of course, much wider than the Arts. We can see the desire to achieve in imaginative ways in a host of everyday situations. Reg's enterprise in making a bed or peeling the potatoes, although laborious, is an example of creativity against the odds. Disabled people can shame many of us who have all our faculties by their determination to leave their mark. This resolve to overcome is made public in the world of sport. For instance the Handicapped Olympics based in Arnhem in 1980 included a blind woman who won the Bowls' championship, a one-legged man who jumped over 7 feet in the High Jump and another man who climbed the Matterhorn in his wheelchair. The sense of personal identity in coping with disability so creatively was brought out by one of the competitors, an American called John who was crippled by polio. When asked, somewhat inanely, by an interviewer whether he would like to be able to walk again, he replied, 'If I couldn't be the person John is, I would want to stay here in this wheelchair.'

3. Sense of humour

In thinking about the place of humour in coping with disability, I am reminded of C.S. Lewis's refreshing view that we can take sex too seriously and that what is needed is a 'roar of old-fashioned laughter'.[6] Handicap, too, can be taken too seriously and there are times, however rare, when a sense of the ridiculous can lighten the load and encourage both sufferer and those around. Let us briefly mention two instances.

The first repertory company that Anna worked with was called the 'Theatre of the Disabled'. This company comprised a collection of women who suffered from a wide range of disabilities and whose ages ran from the early twenties to the fifties. It was the first time that Anna had worked with disabled people and she found the group identity a mixed experience. On the one hand, journalists and interviewers would lump the women together as 'the disabled', concentrating their questions on the *problems* of handicap. On the other hand, the band of women involved developed a sense of camaraderie in which they were able to laugh at themselves. As they wheelchaired their way from one side of the stage to the other during rehearsals they would, on occasions, make fun of being labelled 'cripples'. They would cry out, amidst peels of laughter: 'We're crips: we can't help it!'

It was a similar, though more private, sense of the ridiculous that helped keep me going during the long months of blindness. As I got used to limited vision I found I could help Joy a little in the kitchen. One day, while she was at work and the children at school, I set to with great gusto to deal with a pile of washing up. As I listened to music on the radio, enjoying the warmth of the soapy water and heaping the dishes carefully by the side of the sink, I had a distinct sense of personal worth and usefulness. In my blissful state my hands closed over a substantial, slightly yielding circular object, which must have been resting on one of the larger plates I had just plunged into the bowl. The realisation that I had finger contact with a thoroughly soaked, freshly baked fruit cake, destined for family tea, led to a slightly shocked pause in the flow of my well-meant activity. There was only one way to handle the situation. Give the cake a brief chance to dry on the plate-rack and announce to the children, hot-foot from school, that mum's fruit cake was now a sponge!

God and Weakness

In considering becoming 'old already' we have noted the frustrations that can arise in the disabled through a range of losses. The prime losses we have discussed are those of independence and spontaneity, but we have also referred to the loss of contact with others and the loss of dignity that can be felt where those around are patronising. In all these states of deprivation and weakness, we need to see that our God is a God who also knows deprivation and weakness.

Carlo Carretto, an Italian monk and experienced mountain-climber, was on the receiving end of a ghastly mistake. Just prior to a 600 kilometre trek through an area of the Saharan desert he was given an injection by a friend, a male nurse, that would strengthen him for the journey. Somehow the nurse used the wrong vial, injecting a toxic substance into Carretto's thigh which paralysed his leg permanently within twenty-four hours. He was to spend the next thirty years suffering from a friend's moment of carelessness and, at the same time, demonstrating his conviction that this tragedy is also a means of God's grace. He writes of the God who has himself plumbed the depths to bring to the suffering life's secret:

> Where is the secret? Here it is: God is a crucified God. God
> is the God who allows himself to be defeated, God is the

God who has revealed himself in the poor. God is the God
who has washed my feet, God is Jesus of Nazareth.[7]

Let us spend the last few pages of this chapter thinking how
the 'Crucified God' can bring his solace to, amongst others,
the disabled. He, in his identifying sufferings, has been called
the 'Wounded Healer'.[8] We might also say that in his offering
of himself to the disabling horror of crucifixion he comes, for
us, the 'Handicapped God'. We see here his loss of
independence, loss of spontaneity, loss of contact with others
and loss of dignity.

Jesus knew about a *loss of independence*. It was, in fact, the
mainspring of his life to seek out and obey God's will in every
respect. His trusting dependency on the Father was absolute.
He said to the Jews, 'I do nothing on my own but speak just
what the Father has taught me' (Jn 8:28). This glad obedience
was lived out on the road to Jerusalem, the path of suffering,
the way of the cross.

The word 'handicap', originating as a sporting term ('hand
in the cap' to draw out forfeit money as a wager on a match),
has come to mean 'any encumbrance or disability that weighs
upon effort'.[9] We see the stark handicapping of Jesus as the
impossible burdens of the Garden, the betrayal, the
desertion, the trial, the flogging, the route to Golgotha and
the crucifixion weigh down on him. He knows the fear of
incapacity, a weakness that leads to exhaustion, the
stumbling of powerless legs, the piercing pain of impalation,
the agony of immobilised limbs and the horrors of
asphyxiation. The 'Handicapped God' suffers with those who
battle with cerebral palsy, muscular dystrophy, multiple
sclerosis and all other disabling conditions that imprison the
body and rob us of physical independence.

By the same token, Jesus knows about a *loss of
spontaneity*. His life was coloured by an immediacy in
response to the questions and needs of others. The crossfire of
pharisaic debate, the searchings of a rich young ruler, the love
of a forgiven prostitute, the indignation of perplexed
disciples were all handled with a wisdom and love that was

spontaneous. As he submitted himself on the path to Calvary, he relinquished at least something of his directness. Isaiah 53:7 expresses this graphically:

> He was oppressed and afflicted,
> yet he did not open his mouth;
> he was led like a lamb to the slaughter,
> and as a sheep before her shearers is silent,
> so he did not open his mouth.

Although our Lord's silent submission was voluntary, I believe that those who suffer involuntarily – and are silent or inarticulate through a stroke or other disability – can know he identifies with them in their affliction.

A *loss of contact with others* was supreme in the sequence of deprivation that Jesus endured for us. We see the seeds of isolation in Peter's angry reaction to the Lord's words about his coming death:

> [Jesus] then began to teach them that the Son of Man must suffer many things and be rejected by the elders, chief priests and teachers of the law, and that he must be killed and after three days rise again. He spoke plainly about this, and Peter took him aside and began to rebuke him (Mk 8:31,32).

Later, as Jesus led the way on the road to Jerusalem and certain execution, the fear and puzzlement of the disciples further indicated a potential rift in their relationship with the Lord. (Mk 10:32). This rift widened into a chasm as they all 'deserted him and fled' (Mk 14:50).

Some of his followers, particularly the women, did their best to keep close to him in his hour of need. The small group huddled together at the foot of the cross included his mother. As he hung there above them he must have longed for some physical contact with friends and family. As always his love reached out to the needs of others. He could not embrace his mother or his best friend but they could care for each other. As we have previously noted (page 29), we read:

When Jesus saw his mother there, and the disciple whom
he loved standing near by, he said to his mother, 'Dear
woman, here is your son,' and to the disciple, 'Here is your
mother.' From that time on, this disciple took her into his
home (Jn 19:26,27).

Before the crucifixion, Jesus had predicted that his disciples
would desert him but, at the same time, he was confident of
the Father's continuing presence: 'You will leave me all alone.
Yet I am not alone, for my Father is with me' (Jn 16:32). Even
though his trust in the Father was well-founded, he was still
to know ultimate forsakenness. While he bore the full weight
of humanity's sin, contact with the Father was broken for
three hours of darkness. Such was the Father's remoteness
that Jesus used the less personal word 'God' in his cry of
dereliction: 'My God, my God, why have you forsaken me?'
(Mt 27:46).

It is in this unsurpassed experience of desertion by the only
one who could be completely relied on that Jesus fathomed
the depths of human suffering. There can be no greater loss.
We need to see that, within the loss of contact with other
people which disability often brings, the sufferer need never
fear the Father's absence. The Son was forsaken so that we
might *never* be forsaken.

The final loss that we shall consider in Jesus's suffering is
the *loss of dignity*. The scandal of his trial, the brutality at the
hands of the soldiers, their mock worship of the 'King of the
Jews', the fancy-dress parade in front of Herod and the
degradation of a death reserved for criminals, piled indignity
upon indignity. Something of the dehumanising effect of his
manhandling is brought out in the prophetic words of the
psalmist: 'I am a worm and not a man, scorned by men and
despised by the people' (Ps 22:6) and in the picture of the
Suffering Servant painted in Isaiah 52:14: ' . . . his appearance
was so disfigured beyond that of any man and his form
marred beyond human likeness.'

Again, where the disabled are on the receiving end of
ridicule, spite or condescension they can take heart in the
companionship of the Christ who, though 'despised and

rejected by men', endured the cross 'for the joy set before him'. Further, no loss of dignity, even amongst those who feel acutely their twisted bodies, their shaking limbs, their incomprehensible words, can match the bringing down of our 'Handicapped God'. This is the God who then rises up, shedding all disability in his resurrection power. As we shall see in our last chapter, we too, whatever our affliction, not only partake of his sufferings but will, one day, share in his glory.

In the meantime, let us feel the breadth of the stricken Christ's identifying love in these words of Richard Holloway's:

> Our Lord was identified totally with our experience. We know that one of the meanings of his life was a recapitulation of the whole human experience, of everything that had happened to humanity, only he went through it properly. Every level of abandonment he plumbed. He united himself to it all, to every desolate experience, every forsaken child.[10]

LIVING WITH DYING

I was sure I was dying, and this to me was a cause both of wonder and disquiet

Julian of Norwich

Jonathan and Kate, whom we met in chapter one, were married on a gusty August day in 1985. Friends and family had gathered from far and near to pack the village church, while Upland House, where the couple were to live, awaited the crowds for a reception that was to run into the next day – culminating in an early morning communion service for the undaunted. The grounds of the house were decked with all the trimmings of a truly festive occasion: trestle tables in the barn laden with lovingly prepared food, a large marquee for drinks, speeches and dancing, a bonfire to eat, chat and sing around. And yet, for some, the celebrations were tinged with a sense of pending trouble in the lives of these young, talented newly weds – for a number of the guests knew that Jonathan had cancer and might become seriously ill within the next year or two.

It was just under a year before the wedding that the engaged couple had become aware of the gravity of an enlarged, bleeding mole on Jonathan's back. Operations to remove the offending lump and, subsequently, to dissect away affected glands in the left armpit had been followed by a reasonably active six months or so that had raised hopes that all might be well. However, while on a walking holiday with friends a little before the marriage, Jonathan's normally boundless energy had been clearly limited. Kate, thinking back to her fiancé's symptoms at that time, recalled her tearfulness and the growing conviction 'deep down' that his condition was serious. Nonetheless, they enjoyed their honeymoon, returning to Upland House and the adjustments of married life. These adjustments were unusual in that Kate and Jonathan were part of a joint venture, with another, older couple, to run the property as a guest house. Besides the comparative lack of privacy in this arrangement, the newly weds also faced a brief but, in the circumstances, all too quick, parting. Jonathan had, for some time, been preparing for a non-stipendiary ministry at the local parish church and now, within a few weeks of their honeymoon, he needed to be away from Kate on a pre-ordination retreat.

His absence, though only for one week, was all the more keenly felt by her afterwards when she discovered that he had been battling with an exceptionally intense headache throughout. Now ordained, he returned to Upland House to a night of pain and vomiting, a GP's visit and, a day or two later, an urgent hospital admission. A scan confirmed Kate's worst fears, for Jonathan had developed a secondary growth in the brain and the outlook was extremely bleak.

This time of grim realisation was a mixture of anguish and solace. Kate, who had recently completed a postgraduate training as a nurse, was able to stay in the side ward with Jonathan over the next week. Initially this was a most distressing experience – particularly at nights when he was very confused and she could make no sense of what he was trying to say. A deep-seated fear welled up within her that he would survive this episode only to become a 'non-companion' who would be incoherent and could not communicate.

As Jonathan's treatment by steroids and radiotherapy continued he gradually became more lucid and he and Kate entered a period of closeness and mutual comfort. After a while he improved enough to be home-based, attending the hospital daily for a further three weeks of radiation. Looking back, Kate recalls a very special stretch of time in which they were able to say whatever they wanted to each other. At one level, this included Jonathan sharing his visual hallucinations with her, for the drugs he was on produced, at times, a veritable galaxy of cantering horses and little green men that moved about on the walls of their bedroom. At another level, they were able to pool their thoughts and feelings about the future, Jonathan declaring that he had no fear of death – only of dying, and its prospects of pain and deterioration.

His honesty about what he faced extended to his concern about Kate's outlook. He was keen that she should find fulfilment in earning a living and, on one occasion, said to her, 'It looks as if you've been given another life.' Kate sums up the bittersweet experiences of this time in these words: 'It's as if we needed a crisis to be brought close – we could so easily have carried on without communicating because we lived such busy lives.'

It is as if this month of deep emotional closeness was a gift that would sustain them through the coming months of Jonathan's physical decline – a decline that proceeded stage by stage: loss of hair, inability to walk far, taking to a wheelchair, loss of power to climb the stairs, eating less and less, drinking less and less and, as his body took on skeletal proportions, mental deterioration. It was the stepwise nature of this wasting away that helped Kate cope. She felt that she received just enough strength for each phase, so much so that she found an inner reluctance to come to terms with a particular stage too quickly – because success at one step would mean that the challenge of another step would materialise, as surely as night follows day. One friend remarked that Kate was having to live life 'at a thousand miles an hour', that what for most couples takes fifty years or so had been speeded up, so that marriage, working life, retirement and now terminal illness had been compressed into a mere few months. Jonathan's disease continued its 'fast forward' progression. Just as Kate discovered sufficient strength for each phase so she also found that the rate of change, though breathtaking, was manageable. If the milestones of their life together had flicked past any faster she feels she would not have survived.

Inevitably, given the speed of Jonathan's decline, both he and Kate experienced a wide range of frustrations. By degrees, his physical deterioration spread its tentacles to rob him of even everyday activity so that driving and walking became past pleasures. His deep inner frustration was well controlled but, from time to time, especially in the car with Kate at the wheel, he would cry out in anger. As his body weakened, the impetus to drive and walk lessened and the blows of deprivation were thus softened.

Kate's trials were many and various. Her love for Jonathan, nursing experience and the support of their doctor, friends and family combined into a commitment to care for him at home. With their life as a married couple so fleeting it is small wonder that Jonathan and his every need filled Kate's horizon. At nights he was too restless with discomfort to tolerate her physical closeness and so they decided to sleep separately. This arrangement caused a great deal of sexual frustration for Kate; in time a larger bed in a larger room brought them together again, though Jonathan was too incapacitated to make love.

Both Kate and Jonathan had a wide circle of friends and it was natural, therefore, that the rate of visiting was high. Brian and Mary, who shared Upland House with them, were a great help in handling enquiries on the phone but there were still times when well-intentioned visitors tended to overstay their welcome. Because Jonathan, as he declined in strength, would find his attempts to respond to callers increasingly draining, Kate was obliged to give visitors more of her time. It is not surprising that there were moments of irritation for her in these circumstances when she felt she would rather be with her dying husband. Even so, most who came were sensitive to the situation and brought a measure of love and encouragement with them. Those whose sense of timing was less appropriate might receive a particular ploy from Jonathan during one of his more lucid periods. If the visit was proving too much, he would suddenly say, 'So you've got to go, have you?' and then promptly close his eyes. It would have taken the thickest of skins to resist this hint and stay on!

Given the extremity of their predicament, it is no surprise that Kate and Jonathan wrestled long and hard with the question of healing. What was God's will in their situation? How did he want them to pray? Should they ask for healing? A number of the phone-calls and letters they received were from fellow-Christians who urged them to trust God for health or seek out this or that person with gifts of healing. As they thought and prayed about their quandary they concluded that, primarily, they should look for the Lord's will within the context of one or two groups which would meet regularly for prayer. Twelve noon, every Thursday became a focal point for several bands of faithfully praying people. The vicarage in another parish, where Jonathan had served as a Reader and choir member, was the gathering place for twenty or so villagers who met with him and Kate for a service of laying on of hands. In fact, Jonathan sought the Lord's strengthening on a number of occasions both through having hands laid on him and through anointing with oil, as well as through the more routine praying of countless Christian friends.

Although Kate and Jonathan remained open to the possibility of healing through much of the illness, there were times when it was very difficult to pray for a miracle. God did not seem to be intervening with the spectacular but rather to be answering prayer in a host of other, no less tangible, ways. There grew up between the young couple a sense of timelessness in their relationship, a precious extension of the openness and harmony they had enjoyed during and following the hospital admission. This feel for eternity gave security for the future – come what may – and dispelled anxiety. Each day was to be lived as it came and received with gratitude. As Jonathan grew iller he accepted the reality that he was dying of cancer and, freed from uncertainty, was able to notice and appreciate the simple everyday things of life – a loving smile from Kate, the visit of a close friend, a tastefully served meal.

Undergirding this 'living with dying' was the deep conviction that God was in control and, therefore, all was well. As Kate reminisces, she comments on how struck she was by Jonathan's peacefulness: many others have made the same observation. In spite of his stratagem with the occasional over-persistent visitor, Jonathan was one of those suffering 'missionaries of comfort' who are somehow a tonic to those who call. Kate tells how he would entertain his visitors, laughing and joking with them until he was overcome by tiredness: he would be exhausted, they refreshed.

It was late on in Jonathan's illness that I visited him. As I entered their large sunlit bedroom I was impressed by the room's tranquillity. Jonathan was lying still, his marbled skin barely concealing the bony structure of his wasted body. Somehow Kate and I helped him to the bay window where he was able to lie on bedding, propped up to gaze out over the garden or to doze in the spring sunshine. The three of us talked a little but Jonathan was soon asleep. As we sat there and watched him, the sense of God's peace upon him and, thereby, on us was strong. Kate and I, speaking softly, gradually picked up a conversation while Jonathan slept. Suddenly his head turned towards me, his eyes opened and he asked with gentle courtesy, 'Roger, will you have a sherry? I'm sure Kate will have one.' It was then about eleven in the morning, we had just drunk coffee and, as I glanced at Kate to see how best to reply, we realised he was asleep again. The Lord was manifest in that room of sickness and I left it uplifted by the peace and quiet concern for detail of a dying man.

When Jonathan had emerged into awareness after his hospital admission he had soon, seeing the gravity of his condition, begun to believe that he would not recover and would die quite quickly of the cancer in his brain. He had, in fact, been surprised at how dramatically his headache and vomiting had cleared up as the steroids lessened the fluid around the tumour. Now, five months or so later, he knew that he was living on borrowed time and, to quote his GP, 'each day was a bonus'. His physique had been deteriorating for some time and now he had the added stress of fresh bouts of retching and vomiting. There was no mistaking the message. Jonathan knew he was dying of multiple second-aries.

Kate, backed by the caring support of their doctor and, during the final few weeks, the practical help of a nursing friend, Liz, and Jonathan's brother, James, worked all hours to bring comfort and relief to her dying husband. Due to the persistence of vomiting and pain, Jonathan needed to have regular injections. Round about the middle of May, seeing no improvement in his illness and anticipating a long and distressing haul ahead, it seems he became resigned to the fact that the end of his suffering could not be far away. One evening soon after, while Kate was giving him an injection, he said softly but distinctly, 'I want to die.' From then on, so his wife felt, Jonathan willed himself into the next world.

Six days later he slipped into unconsciousness, and Kate bed-bathed and shaved him for the last time. That night was one of many that Kate and Liz slept on a mattress on the floor, taking it in turns to attend to Jonathan. Kate, though aware that the end was near, was too exhausted to keep awake. Soon after four in the morning Liz woke her friend. Jonathan had just died. The two women sobbed in each other's arms, woke James, and the three, who had spent so much time at Jonathan's bedside in recent weeks, cried together till the sun was well up and the rest of the house was stirring.

The sense of Jonathan's presence lingered on in the room. His body was laid out on the bed and Kate and Liz continued to sleep in close attendance until the funeral four days later. Their immediate tears had released a great deal of pent-up emotion and now, as they tidied the room and chatted together, they had a vivid feeling of Jonathan watching them lovingly and laughing at their antics. Some weeks later, Kate recalls, she needed to bring to mind his stubbly growth of hair and other individual features of his appearance. Four months after his death, she shared how she was aware of his presence at a less physical level and more in her thinking and feeling. She would wonder what thoughts he would have about her decisions, how he would feel about a particular plan of action, respond to her encounters with other people or react to new places she was visiting. At times his influence seemed so important that she could see there was a danger she might even pray to him. As more time passed, Kate found that, though Jonathan's projected views were still crucial, she was increasingly freed to discover and respond to God's way forward into her own future.

I have given Kate and Jonathan's story in considerable detail for two main reasons. First, because, to quote Alastair Campbell 'Listening to stories touches levels of feeling and experience which the intellect cannot entertain'[1]: the account of two young people 'living with dying' can move us to a depth of understanding that endless theorising cannot. And second, their experience, nonetheless, illustrates and fleshes out some key principles that can help others of us as we, or our loved ones, face dying, death and bereavement.

Responses to Dying

There are few if any who actually *like* the idea of dying. Some may long for oblivion but most are appalled at the process of getting there. Alexander Solzhenitsyn explores this horror of decline in his Nobel Prize-winning book *Cancer Ward*. Here Vadim, facing death himself at the age of twenty-six, makes this comment on Rusanov, a fellow-patient who had been a 'good solid worker all his life': 'He was not frightened of dying "one day", he was frightened of dying now.'[2] It is this fear of dying in the here and now which makes death a taboo subject – a taboo that can only be breached by many through humour. Woody Allen's 'throw away' lines: 'It's not that I'm afraid to die. I just don't want to be there when it happens' are a classic example of the attempt to dismiss fear through laughter.

Dr Elizabeth Kübler-Ross acknowledges this fear of death in the first chapter of her book *On Death and Dying*, and then goes on to explore the chain of reactions which often accompany the resolution of that fear in the dying person. We have already noted many aspects of responding – numbness, anger, anxiety, depression – as we have considered those who face acute or chronic illness. In fact, as we have also seen, there is a certain pattern in trying to cope with any serious loss, whether of work, mobility, sight, hearing or general health. The prospect of ultimate loss – the loss of life itself – leads to a similar sequence, whose intensity varies with the rapidity and nature of bodily and mental deterioration. We will look at Dr Kübler-Ross's five stages of reaction to dying by way of summary, also referring the reader back to our fuller sections on anger (pp. 36ff.) and depression (pp. 45ff.). In clarifying these phases we need to appreciate that each individual's response to dying is unique. For some the sequences are clear cut, for most the transitions are blurred and reaction moves to and fro between the different stages.

1. Denial

It has been well said that 'neither the sun nor death can be looked at with a steady eye.'[3] As when the glare of the full sun suddenly hits a driver's eyes, one of the first reactions to dying is to look away. Here there are elements of 'No, not me!' 'Dying is something which happens to others', 'There must be some mistake.' Sometimes this denial of reality is extremely persistent and a patient may accuse hospital staff of mixing up pathology lab. reports and misreading X-rays, and may seek a series of further medical opinions in a search for a doctor who will give a clean bill of health.

However it is important to see that some degree of numbness and denial is not only normal but serves the valuable function of protecting those concerned from being crushed by a burden which can be too quickly shouldered. Those who seek to help people cope with terminal illness – both the afflicted and those who look on – should remember the value of the buffering effect of shock and numbness. Most will begin to accept the truth in their own time. In other words, the carer needs to be wary of either forcing the pace

('You *must* accept what the doctor has said; you *are* dying, you know') or lagging behind the sufferer's courage in wanting to be frank about the facts ('I want now to think through exactly what it means for me to face death').

2. Anger

As the truth sinks in, the 'No, not me!' of denial becomes the 'Why me?' of protest and anger. There are many aspects to this angry questioning. At heart, it is often the *loss of control* that is particularly galling. We all love a measure of independence and the relinquishment of the freedom to come and go, to pick and choose, is something most will resist. The frustration for the young and fit, whose lives should normally stretch for decades before them, is especially intense. Jonathan's angry outbursts when Kate had to take over the wheel of their car were not at her but at his own incapacity. Similarly, her own dilemmas, over the well-meaning visits of friends, the gathering round Jonathan of groups of praying Christians and the question of admission or continued caring at home, related to the threat of a loss of control – the loss of influence over the last vestige of their all too brief life together.

Anger is an untidy emotion: it has to spill over in one direction or another. In fact, if an attempt is made to ignore it, it often perversely oversteps itself in a variety of directions. Doctors are blamed for incompetence, nurses for heavy-handedness, home-helps for intrusiveness, fellow-Christians for insensitivity, family and friends for either overdoing or underdoing their affection and caring. God may be the long-stop who is ultimately meant to field all the anger.

These strong negative feelings can give those who try to help the patient a rough ride. The sufferer is seen as difficult, perverse or ungrateful and there is danger of a wall of resentment building up between the carers and the cared for. Here, perhaps more than at any other stage, there is a necessity for compassionate listening. Dr Kübler-Ross, writing in a hospital context, is aware that we need to know something of our own anxieties if we are to give our attention effectively to the angry feelings of those who suffer:

> We have to learn to listen to our patients and at times even to accept some irrational anger, knowing that the relief in expressing it will help them toward a better acceptance of the final hours. We can do this only when we have faced our own fears of death, our own destructive wishes, and have become aware of our own defenses which may interfere with our patient care.[4]

3. Bargaining

As the question 'Why me?' becomes less pressing, the patient may begin to make the request 'Help me!' Frequently, according to Kübler-Ross, one or two propositions are put in God's direction, for example: 'God, if you'll get me out of hospital, I'll live a better life' or 'God, I promise I'll attend church regularly if you'll heal me of this illness.'

This bargaining counter is not unlike that produced by a child who says, 'Mum, if I wash up – *and* dry up – at every meal this week, can I stay late at Amanda's party on Saturday?' The conditional offer may prove irresistible to Mum but a wise parent will not enter into such a negotiation with a son or daughter. Caring and responsible behaviour should not depend on successful bartering. Similarly, as we shall see more fully later in this chapter, attempts at 'death-bed' bargaining with God, though understandable, threaten to devalue the patient's relationship with God. God's lordship demands of us unconditional obedience and his compassion is wider than our small-minded manoeuvres give him credit for.

4. Depression

As we saw in chapter two, depression is frequently associated with a sense of loss; and so it is not surprising that the person who faces the loss of life itself commonly becomes depressed at some stage or other. Kübler-Ross helpfully distinguishes two forms of depression in the dying person:

(a) Reactive depression

Here there is a depressed reaction to the circumstances that surround the patient. He or she will need to talk freely and may be reassured where the situation can, to some extent, be rectified. A mother may be distressed at the lack of provision for her children but will find relief as husband, friends and social worker begin to find solutions; a working man may become depressed about his job until a colleague assures him that his work can be covered by others; a woman may suffer deeply a sense of the loss of her femininity following the removal of a breast for cancer but can also readjust when her feelings are understood, and her physical appearance and self-esteem are re-established by the fitting of a prosthesis.

(b) Preparatory depression

Later in the course of a fatal illness, there comes a type of depression which is essential in preparing the patient for coming death. Whereas reactive depression in this context is readily recognised because the sufferer wants to talk, the preparatory form is easily overlooked because the dying person may resort to silence. In fact, this silence is often desperately needed. The patient is seeking the space to face the grim reality of imminent death. Visitors who insist on talking – particularly if they assail the patient with a battery of questions – may prevent that quiet reflection which can strengthen for the days ahead. What is necessary, rather, is the stillness which can come out of a true companionship, where those that care can 'sit where they sit', content to reassure within the silence with a smile or gentle touch.

5. Acceptance

The final stage of facing death, as we saw with Jonathan, is an acceptance of its reality and inevitability. As Kate observed, Jonathan, about a fortnight before he died, began to welcome the end and the release it afforded. Even so, long before that he knew that he was dying of cancer and was resigned to that eventuality.

This period of acceptance is an extension of preparatory depression and often includes an increased tendency to sleep and a desire to be left alone. Any inclination to keep up with the events and changes in people's lives, as well as with more general news, may lapse. The newspaper is unread, radio and television are off. This can be an upsetting time for friends and the wider family since their visits may be too disruptive for the patient.

However it is important that closer loved ones see that they can still play a quietly supportive role. Dr Kübler-Ross makes the point well in the context of a brief visit:

> Our presence may just confirm that we are going to be around until the end. We may just let him know that it is all right to say nothing when the important things are taken care of and it is only a question of time until he can close his eyes forever. It may reassure him that he is not left alone when he is no longer talking and a pressure of the hand, a look, a leaning back in the pillows may say more than many 'noisy' words.[5]

It is with respect to these later stages of 'living with dying' that the Hospice Movement is providing an excellent alternative to conventional care at home or hospital for people with terminal cancer (and perhaps, in time, for other terminal illnesses), to 'die with dignity'.[6] The movement offers several models of caring, including admission to a bedded unit, the provision of facilities for advice and meeting others at a day centre and the support of patient and family in their own home by a 'home care' team of nursing sisters, backed by doctor, social worker and voluntary assistants. Whichever approach is adopted, the high ratio between those who care and the cared for, the ample time made available for those in need to relate fully to the helpers, and the commitment to prevent pain, all encourage the sufferer, and the relations, to reach a realistic level of acceptance.

In this chapter, in telling the story of Kate and Jonathan, we have been thinking about 'living with dying', seeking to clarify the stages of loss as described by Kübler-Ross. I want us, finally to turn our attention to the question of whether the Bible can throw any light on the grieving process and so, hopefully, find further help for those of us who battle, in one way or another, with fatal illness and its consequences. We could look in many places for the Scriptures have much to say about dying well, as well as the reality of death and life beyond the grave. We will pick up these themes in our last chapter but, for the moment, I would like to concentrate on a particular section of the Bible which illuminates human reaction to loss; the *psalms of lament*.

Psalms of Lament

Many of us in times of uncertainty, distress or puzzlement, find ourselves turning to the Psalter, for it is here that all human experience is unfolded and all human emotion is bared. Some have felt moved by the psalms because of a 'companionship of feelings' with the psalmist.[7] Others have stressed the way the structure of a psalm can help the individual or group in their response to God. Amongst the latter, Professor Donald Capps has demonstrated how the form of the psalms of lament can aid the process of grieving.

He points out that there are many types of psalm in the Psalter – psalms of penitence, songs of thanksgiving and praise, songs of trust, wisdom psalms – but the psalms of lament outnumber all other varieties, comprising over a third of the total. These psalms of lament were songs of mourning for either personal or communal use and, Capps argues, have a structure that, in some ways, parallels the stages of grief as outlined by Dr Kübler-Ross and others. However, without criticising the value of the work of Kübler-Ross and other researchers, Capps writes that 'contemporary stage theories of grief and dying differ most from the lament' in their tendency to leave out the 'transforming intervention' of God.[8]

Let us look then, at four of the six key elements in the psalms of lament to find how the Lord's 'transforming intervention' can help the person who is 'living with dying'.

1. Complaint

Following an 'address to God', the psalmist cries out in anguish about the problem he faces, whether illness, the ravages of sin, the betrayal of friends, the threat of enemies or the fear of death. In Psalm 102:4,5, for example, an afflicted man bemoans his fate:

> My heart is blighted and withered like grass;
> I forget to eat my food;
> Because of my loud groaning
> I am reduced to skin and bones.

His anorexia and weight loss, along with the taunting of his foes (verse 8), are seen as results of God's judgment – 'because of your great wrath, for you have taken me up and thrown me aside' (verse 10). At other times there is, rather than Psalm 102's sense of guilt, an element of outrage. In Psalm 13, David's anger is levelled at God:

> How long, O Lord? Will you forget
> me for ever?
> How long will you hide your face
> from me? (Ps 13:1).

Further, we see, especially in the so-called 'cursing' psalms, protestations of innocence; in Psalm 59:4, for instance, David declares, 'I have done no wrong.'

These examples give just three of the psalmists' states of mind as they deliver their complaints: guilt, anger and self-justification – and it is these feelings, in particular, that are often the hallmark of the person who faces the death of someone close. One, with a heavy conscience at the progressive deterioration of a loved one, might say, 'I feel so guilty that we'd just had a row. I said so many hurtful things ... When I came back he was already unconscious and now I fear there will be no chance to make amends;' another, caring for a friend who is fatally ill, might cry out, 'I feel so angry that she's dying so young. What a waste of talent and potential!' and a third, looking on at a relative's dying, might declare, 'Nobody can accuse *me* of neglect; I'm doing all I can.'

Those of us who confront dying and death, whether for ourselves or in the experience of others, can take heart from the psalmists' complaints. We see in them the expression of a welter of emotions in the face of affliction and in the presence of a living and holy God. Even the negative feeling which goes beyond anger – the cry for vengeance – is given words within the Psalter. However else we understand the 'curses' of such psalms as 35, 59, 70 and 109, we should be encouraged that, as we seek to cope with illness and its fatal outcome, no complaint is out of bounds before our understanding Lord.

It is as we declare our anger, guilt, feelings of innocence, and vindictiveness that, to follow Capps' stages, we may come to a 'confession of trust'. Such proclamations of belief that God can provide in the midst of adversity are a frequent theme of the psalms of lament. For example, in Psalm 71:5 we read,

> For you have been my hope, O
> Sovereign Lord,
> my confidence since my youth,

and in Psalm 139:17,

> How precious to me are your
> thoughts, O God!
> How vast is the sum of them!

We have seen something of this confidence in the story of Kate and Jonathan where, in the middle of their frustration and anger, they were able to acknowledge their trust in the God who ordered their ways.

For some, though, hurtful emotions against God and

others can harden into set attitudes of bitterness or an unforgiving spirit. Here legitimate complaint can, in time, fossilise into resentment. Any 'confession of trust' is steadily resisted, for such a sufferer does not seem to want to find any relief from a vicious circle of blaming others and pitying the self. This is a route that the afflicted and those concerned for them need not follow, as God is always waiting in love for the simplest step of trust to be taken. Even in the bleakest of the psalms of lament, there is a glimmer of hope as the psalmist at least looks Godwards in the middle of his anguish. In Psalm 38, for instance, David acknowledges,

> All my longings lie open before you,
> O Lord;
> my sighing is not hidden from you (Ps 38:9).

In our caring for those who face dying and grief we should always remember that, amidst the needs for the sufferer to complain angrily to God and others, small stirrings of faith can begin. Sometimes, it is the one who shows God's love as he or she listens that can help initiate a 'confession of trust'. In effect, the needy one says, 'I am angry, guilty and feel wronged. Yet your taking me seriously helps me trust you. That trust, in turn, I feel encourages me to start trusting God too, however hesitantly...'

2. Petition

And so, following the 'address to God', the 'complaint' and the 'confession of trust', it is natural for the psalmist to turn to prayer. Such petitions abound in the psalms of lament: 'Turn, O Lord, and deliver me' (Ps 6:4); 'O Lord, do not forsake me' (Ps 38:21); 'O Lord, have mercy on me' (Ps 41:4); 'Relent, O Lord! How long will it be? Have compassion on your servants' (Ps 90:13).

It is here that Donald Capps' analysis raises questions over Elizabeth Kübler-Ross's idea of 'bargaining'. Although it is undoubtedly true that many in need do try to bargain with

God, there is a danger that the heartfelt prayer behind the apparent attempt to manipulate the Almighty is unrecognised by the carers. It is probably best for all of us who seek to encourage the afflicted to see that a patient's plea, 'God, if you will heal me, then I will...' is, in fact, a cry for help. In effect, they may be saying. 'God, please take away my guilt, anger, self-pity, heaviness of heart... Bring your healing to my attitudes as well as my body... Strengthen me to face the future.'

It is understandable that many will try to trade with God in their petitions – partly because his bounty towards them can scarcely be believed ('There must be a snag somewhere! What ploy can I offer to make sure of his favour?') and partly because there is a sneaky feeling that he *does* demand something of them ('Christians say he wants to be Lord of the whole of my life. Wouldn't a "trade off" of, say, more regular church attendance be an easier option?'). In fairness though, we all have to admit to mixed motives in our praying. It is God who can see through our conflicts to the heart's desire of our fumbling requests.

3. Words of assurance

In response to the psalmists' petitions we find words of assurance which are at the very centre of God's 'transforming intervention'. The psalms provide innumerable examples of this turning-point from prayer to praise, where the singer rehearses the wonders of God's hand upon him. We see this, for instance, in Psalm 73:24-26 when Asaph addresses God with these words:

> You guide me with your counsel,
> and afterwards you will take me into glory.
> Whom have I in heaven but you?
> And earth has nothing I desire
> beside you.
> My flesh and my heart may fail,
> but God is the strength of my heart
> and my portion for ever.

For those whose lot is 'living with dying' these 'words of assurance' may come by many means. For Kate and Jonathan they came through God's read and spoken Word, in answer to prayer, through the bread and wine, the laying on of hands, anointing with oil, the counsel of spiritual advisers and the practical caring of friends and family.

In our concern for those who grieve their progressive loss of health we should exercise great sensitivity over 'words of assurance'. It is worth pointing out that, in the structure of the psalms of lament, they come after the petition. It is only as people have begun to turn their complaints into prayers and have found a measure of trust in God that statements of consolation can have their place. We need to avoid the glibness of premature attempts at reassurance: declarations that 'God is love' or 'God understands', though true, do not do much for those who feel resentful at sudden illness or are perplexed by an untimely death.

Often support is given to the needy when we share in their requests to God. Some of the greatest assurances of hope in Christ came to Joy and me when others gathered to pray for us for healing of my blindness. Sometimes, it is simply the presence of one who cares in the name of the Lord that encourages the grieving person to pray, and so find new confidence. Donald Capps tells the story of Harry, whose wife had died of cancer ten weeks or so before his pastor's second visit following the funeral. During the service, Harry had felt bitter about the minister's choice of the passage in John that talks of Jesus sending 'another Comforter'. Now, over two months later and in spite of his earlier resistance, he was experiencing first hand something of God's comforting love. Capps records how Harry asked the pastor: 'Reverend, would it be all right if I prayed and thanked God for his comfort while you're here? *It's easier to think of him when you're around.*'[9]

Perhaps that is the core of the assurance that we can bring to those who suffer. It would be good if we made it our prayer that the afflicted could say of us, 'It's easier to think of him when you're around.'

4. Vow to praise

The outcome of many grieving experiences, as Kübler-Ross states, is an acceptance of the reality of dying and death. Tragically, for those who die without hope in Christ, such acceptance may be little more than a dispirited resignation that life is slipping away and the end of everything personal is at hand. In contrast, the psalms of lament are completed at a high point by a 'vow to praise':

> Praise be the Lord, the God of Israel,
> from everlasting to everlasting.
> Amen and Amen (Ps 41:13).

> One thing God has spoken,
> two things have I heard:
> that you, O God, are strong,
> and that you, O Lord, are loving (Ps 62:11,12).

> But as for me, it is good to be near God.
> I have made the Sovereign Lord my refuge;
> I will tell of all your deeds (Ps 73:28).

Miss Rowland, at the age of eighty-eight and living in sheltered accommodation, looks back at her childhood – when her mother died and she was brought up by various aunts – and a life of recurring illness. Although she is unhappy at her need to rely on others to do her shopping and jobs around the bungalow, and cannot see to sew properly, she is grateful for the care and attention of two brothers, a number of friends, a home-help, the district nurse, her GP and the curate from a nearby church. She faces the future with a 'vow to praise', declaring that she looks forward to death and that, though every night she feels could be her last this side of glory, she leaves the timing and circumstances to her Lord.

And yet there are some who, whether they are 88 or 28, find that their situation is such that they cannot, in all honesty,

turn their minds to praise and thanksgiving. This may be
particularly so for those who look on at the dying of their own
kith and kin. One woman in her early forties, who lives not far
from us, watched a year ago her own daughter die of a
wasting disease in her early teens; she now faces her own
death from cancer and has said recently, 'I don't care what
happens to me; nothing could be worse than seeing June die.'
In a different type of example, I was struck by an entry in the
Guardian, following a disaster in a Dhaka refugee camp
when nearly 20,000 Bihari Muslims were made homeless by
fire:

> 'When the fire got put out, I went to my hut to see if I
> could salvage anything. I got only two things – the bodies
> of my wife and my son,' Fazlur Ralman, aged 32 said.
> 'God is somehow unkind to me.'[10]

Neither June's mother nor the grieving Bihari were in a
position where praising God seemed remotely possible. Such
might, in time, be able to move from their profound anguish
to trust, prayer, assurance and even thanksgiving. However,
many do not. Perhaps they remain puzzled by God's hand on
their lives, perhaps their burden is too heavy for them to look
heavenwards, perhaps their pain or other incapacity is too
overwhelming. Whatever the factors which make the 'vow to
praise' so elusive, such can still find a measure of comfort in
that God also laments. It has been said that 'the God of wrath
is also the God who mourns.'[11] We see the 'lament of God'
portrayed in the prophetic writings of Isaiah, Jeremiah and
Hosea, reaching its climax of identification with afflicted
humanity in the Servant passages, where we read of the One
who is to come – 'a man of sorrows, and familiar with
suffering' (Is 53:3).

And so, where dying and death are faced squarely, we may
at times find praise on our lips to the Sovereign Lord who,
even within our adversity, orders all things well. At other
times we may feel too crushed to sing or give thanks; it is then
we may meet with the God who grieves and mourns with us.

Donald Capps points to this divine 'feeling with' those who confront great loss when he writes that God seems to say to such, 'If I were in your shoes, and you in mine, I would have difficulty praising you.'[12]

HOME AT LAST

Christ has turned all our sunsets into dawns
Clement of Alexandria

If I were ever to be offered that opportunity of the famous – to appear on *Desert Island Discs* – one of the eight records I would choose would be of Schubert's quartet 'Death and the Maiden'. I never fail to be stirred by, in particular, the slow second movement, which is a set of five variations on his song of the same name. When I saw that BBC2 was putting on a film of the Ballet Rambert performing the first two movements of the quartet, I made sure I had a free evening. I was not disappointed. The choreographer, Robert North, had worked out a stunning sequence in which four men and four women – the lead pair in black, the rest in shades of grey – danced out the drama of the claim of death on a young woman. The whole piece demonstrated powerfully the Maiden's ambivalence towards Death. We saw her, at times, cowering before Death, who struck at her with kniving and scything movements; in other episodes, the Maiden swooned at Death's embrace and caresses, or nodded in acceptance towards the black-clad male dancer. At one point another woman dancer tried to comfort the Maiden by coming between her and Death. As the piece concluded, Death prevailed, and the remaining dancers fell back in acquiescence at the Maiden's fate.

We have seen something of this double theme of death being both feared and welcomed throughout this book. Lady

Julian of Norwich, the fourteenth-century solitary, faced death in her thirty-first year and wrote, 'I was sure I was dying, and this to me was a cause both of wonder and disquiet.'[1] These ambivalent attitudes to dying and death – fear and welcome, disquiet and wonder – are symptomatic of the in-between age we live in. We long for wholeness and face illness; we reach out for strength and experience weakness; we look for victory and find defeat; we hope for glory and have to live with shame. And yet, for those who meet with Christ, the road of sorrow is also the path of joy. We discover that the 'here and now' is invaded by eternity and that today's existence can reach into the heavenlies.

These themes of suffering and healing can be seen in terms of our present mortality and our future immortality. In 1 Corinthians 15: 42-44 Paul, having argued the centrality of Christ's resurrection for the Christian faith, now declares the transformation promised to every believer:

> So it will be with the resurrection of the dead. The body that is sown is perishable, it is raised imperishable; it is sown in dishonour, it is raised in glory; it is sown in weakness, it is raised in power; it is sown a natural body, it is raised a spiritual body.

Let us then take these contrasting dimensions as the basis for our thinking as we examine the interweaving strands of suffering and healing in the light of the dying and rising again of our Lord. We find here that our day to day lives are marked by weakness and dishonour (or shame), and our eternal life is distinguished by power and glory.

Theme of Suffering

From time to time in this book we have been reminded of the picture of Jesus as the Servant who identifies completely with the sufferings of those he came to save. Within Isaiah's classic fifty-third chapter the coming Messiah is described in these terms:

He was oppressed and afflicted,
yet he did not open his mouth;
he was led like a lamb to the slaughter,
and as a sheep before her shearers is silent,
so he did not open his mouth (Isa 53:7).

It is this comparison of Christ to a lamb about to be killed
that can give us valuable insight into the path of affliction.
We will keep this imagery in mind as we explore the
hallmarks of the theme of suffering in the 'here and now':
weakness and *shame*.

1. Weakness

If one tried to think hard of something that might represent
vulnerability and weakness within the pastoral lifestyle of the
Old Testament, it is difficult to envisage a more appropriate
symbol than a lamb. Those of us who have enjoyed spring
holidays in mountainous districts, or who live in sheep-
farming country, will be aware of the almost indecent haste
with which lambs will bee-line for their mothers' rear
quarters, to find a tail-quivering solace in milk and animal
warmth. Some years ago while on holiday, I parked my small,
white Ford on the verge of a lonely Highland road to admire
the view. Without realising it, I had separated a ewe from her
new born lamb. The lamb could hear her mother's bleating
from the far side of the car and rushed beneath the tail end of
the vehicle to seek comfort from a hot exhaust pipe!

And yet, this overall image of helplessness is the picture
God's Spirit gives of Jesus Christ, the Lamb of God. Born of a
teenage Jewish girl amidst the smells and sounds of an
animals' feeding place, he took upon himself our frail and
susceptible humanity. In Luke 2:51 we catch a glimpse of him
at the age of twelve, though clearly conscious of God's call,
submitting, nevertheless, to his parents' direction. The writer
to the Hebrews picks up the wider theme of our Lord's
commitment to obey his heavenly Father:

During the days of Jesus' life on earth, he offered up
prayers and petitions with loud cries and tears to the one
who could save him from death, and he was heard
because of his reverent submission. Although he was a
son, he learned obedience from what he suffered (Heb
5:7,8).

It is, supremely, in the dying of Christ that we see the
vulnerability of his human life exposed for all to witness. The
'loud cries and tears' which accompanied his prayers in the
Garden 'to the one who could save him from death', the
betrayal with a kiss, the scattering of panic-stricken friends,
his silence, 'like a lamb to the slaughter', before the high priest
and Herod, the mockery and beating at the hands of Pilate's
soldiers, the stumbling on the way to the cross and the cruel
and lonely death of crucifixion – all speak eloquently of how
far Jesus was prepared to go on the path of weakness, which
was also the path of obedience.

We too are called to the path of weakness, which is the path
of obedience. Just as Paul declares that Christ 'was crucified
in weakness' (2 Co 13:4) he also tells of his own resolve in
coming to the church in Corinth, to know nothing while he
was with them, 'except Jesus Christ and him crucified'. He
writes, 'I came to you in weakness and fear, and with much
trembling' (1 Co 2:3), and later, his words now touched with
irony, 'We are fools for Christ, but you are so wise in Christ!
We are weak, but you are strong! You are honoured, we are
dishonoured!' (1 Co 4:10).

Most of us, if we are honest, despise weakness, particularly
in the moral sphere. We criticise weak attitudes, actions,
decisions, policies. We might say of someone who seems to
spend life dithering and holding back, 'He's really quite
pathetic, so spineless, so weak ... He wouldn't say "Boo!" to a
goose' or, of a faltering government, 'What a hopelessly weak
bunch they are ... It's about time we had an election and got a
group in with some drive and moral fibre.'

In fact, such weakness, which is a lack of resolve and single-
mindedness, is a long way from the vulnerability which Christ

displayed, and his people are called to. The one who 'humbled himself and became obedient to death – even death on a cross!' (Php 2:8) was far from weak in terms of the hardest path of all, the path of yielding in all things to the Father's will. The Greek word *astheneia*, translated as 'weakness', has, in its scriptural use, been defined as describing the 'full range of physical, emotional, social, economic and even spiritual incapacity'.[2] It is a wide-sweeping term, used variously; but, with respect to our Lord's weakness, it seems to emphasise his willing 'self-emptying' as he took on the circumstances of deprivation in an obedient human life and death.

Christ's way, the path of weakness, the path of obedience, is a way of submission to God and service to others. Richard Foster sums up well this costly, but life-giving, journey which Jesus took on our behalf:

> Jesus shattered the customs of His day when He lived out the cross-life by taking women seriously and by being willing to meet with children. He lived the cross-life when He took a towel and washed the feet of His disciples. This Jesus who easily could have called down a legion of angels to His aid chose instead the cross-death of Calvary. Jesus' life was the cross-life of submission and service. Jesus' death was the cross-death of conquest by suffering.[3]

How are we to understand Christ's example, and the same perspectives put across by Paul for Christ's followers? What does the call to the path of weakness and obedience say to those of us who battle daily with illness, handicap, dying and death?

First, we all need to admit our weakness and incapacity. In the physical realm, this may be something many of us have to do daily! We cannot hide from ourselves or others the evidences of wasted, pain-racked bodies, misshapen limbs or extreme lassitude and exhaustion. Others of us, of course, work quite hard at hiding our frailty. I remember, during my twelve months or so of blindness, becoming quite adept at seemingly focusing my gaze at just about the right distance, so that a speaker felt he or she was holding me in rapt attention – and, if a stranger, might then be surprised to learn I was blind.

When we are on the receiving end of unwellness and disability, it is not that most of us wish to deceive (though as we have seen the defence of 'denial', in which there is, in effect, self-deception, has its usefulness for a while) so much as we do not want to burden others unnecessarily. Their cheery 'How are you?' is more often part of the ritual of social contact than a carefully gauged enquiry which expects a full clinical history! The sufferer who insists on telling all will soon find the questions stop flowing.

However, whether we are well or ill, we should face up to something deeper. As Paul Tournier has written:

> All men, in fact, are weak. All are weak because all are afraid. They are all afraid of being trampled underfoot. They are all afraid of their inner weaknesses being discovered. They all have secret faults... They are all afraid of other men and of God, of themselves, of life and of death.[4]

Our need is to confront the reality. We *are* weak, though we like to appear strong – to ourselves, to others, to God. Our inner weaknesses and secret faults are of course fully known to God, and there is no mileage in trying to hide them from him. Our crippling fear of exposure can evaporate if we will allow ourselves to see something of God's compassion and gentleness towards us. His Son, though sinless, lived and died in weakness, so that we, confessing our own weaknesses, might receive forgiveness for the countless ways we have fallen short. Thus we can begin and continue the path of obedience – a path on which we find strength in acknowledged weakness. As Hebrews 4:15,16 says of Jesus and our way forward:

> For we do not have a high priest who is unable to

sympathise with our weaknesses, but we have one who has been tempted in every way, just as we are – yet was without sin. Let us then approach the throne of grace with confidence, so that we may receive mercy and find grace to help us in our time of need.

2. Shame

The pictures of Jesus Christ as Suffering Servant and Lamb of God are not only ones of helplessness but also of dishonour. The Greek word *atimia* has the notion of a 'deprivation of a citizen's rights'. Here there is a stripping of honour from the individual which leaves him or her shamefully exposed. This exposure leads to ridicule and rejection, as portrayed in Isaiah 53:3:

> He was despised and rejected of men, a
> man of sorrows, and familiar with suffering.
> Like one from whom men hide their faces
> he was despised, and we esteemed him not.

Moreover, in Psalm 22:6 we see that the one whose sufferings are foretold experiences shame both within: 'I am a worm and not a man', and without: 'scorned by men and despised by the people'. This double ignominy is fulfilled in the mockery of the crowd and the desertion by the Father as Christ dies a criminal's death – and, in so doing, bears the unbearable, the sins of the whole of fallen humanity from its first rebellion to the last trumpet.

Here is a great mystery – for the Holy One, fully God and fully human, is, to quote Galatians 3:13, made 'a curse for us'. He chooses the way of the cross and is spreadeagled shamefully before us all, aware of his own degradation ('I am a worm and not a man'), despised and taunted by the onlookers and bereft of the Father's companionship. Under the old Mosaic law, anyone who was guilty of a capital offence was, after execution, fixed to a stake or 'hung on a tree' to symbolise God's rejection.[5] When Christ died on a

Roman gallows a parallel sense of shame surrounded him, but with the profoundest of differences. Whereas such a death was traditionally a 'curse' upon the guilty, in *his* death he was made 'a curse for *us*': the 'curse' that was our due, because of our failure to keep God's law in every aspect (Gal 3:10), was laid on him. As Paul puts it in 2 Corinthians 5:21, in words too profound for further comment: 'God made him who had no sin to be sin for us, so that in him we might become the righteousness of God.'

Just as we are called to an awareness of our weakness and vulnerability as we consider Jesus, the Lamb of God, so we are invited to share the shame of the one who was made 'a curse for us'. In Hebrews 13:13 we are summoned to join him 'outside the camp', in his isolation and ostracisation, 'bearing the disgrace (reproach, insult), he bore'. This identification with Jesus will bring upon us a measure of the rejection he suffered, at the hands of people who scorn those who stand apart in obedience to God. And yet, we are 'blessed' (fortunate, blissfully happy) if we are 'insulted because of the name of Christ' (1 Pe 4:14) or, more fully, 'when people insult... persecute... and falsely say all kinds of evil against [us]' became of our loyalty to Christ (Mt 5:11).

So far we have considered the shame and dishonour which can be ours as we align ourselves with the one who was 'despised and rejected of men'. It may be useful now to widen the discussion because our everyday experience of shame is rarely as uncluttered as that. Dick Keyes, in his book *Beyond Identity*, seeks to clarify certain aspects of shame by distinguishing it from guilt. He writes, 'Just as guilt is a falling short of moral norms or commandments, shame is a falling short of our models, our sense of what it is to be heroic.'[6] By 'models' and our sense of the 'heroic' he is referring to those people, ideas and ideals with which we identify. And so, for example, if a young cricketer who plays for a local club aspires to be an Ian Botham then he will be covered in shame every time, in attempting a six, he is caught out easily. Again, where a woman sees herself as a valiant fighter for a feminist perspective, she will feel ashamed if she keeps missing

opportunities to speak out against sexism. Keyes sums up this
view of shame in these words: 'This suffering of shame
therefore is more a fall from ourselves, a blow to our pride in
our own heroism than it is a fall from obedience to God.'[7] He
argues that, usually, we do not need forgiveness for our
shame. Rather, what we long for, and can receive, is God's
full acceptance of us in our embarrassment and confusion.
We observe something of this bounty towards us as we are
welcomed unequivocally by the Lord into his family: 'Both
the one who makes men holy and those who are made holy
are of the same family. So Jesus is not ashamed to call them
brothers' (Heb 2:11).

It is here that we can see that our experience of shame is
often a mixed one. If our 'model' is Christ himself then we will
discover at least three aspects to our sense of dishonour.
There will be many times when we are covered in shame
because we have fallen short of God's standards; here our
shamefacedness will often be rightly tinged with a sense of
guilt, and we will turn to him for fresh forgiveness. On other
occasions, to use Dick Keyes' phrase, we will feel bad because
of a 'fall from ourselves', a sense of catching ourselves out –
and then we can be reminded that Christ understands and is
'not ashamed' to call us brothers and sisters. At other times
we will know something of reproach from others, simply
because we belong to Christ and seek to follow him.

What does all this say to us as we search for his way in the
midst of illness, disability and dying? We find that, within
suffering too, our shame can, in its broad parallel to what the
Suffering Servant went through, be both inner experience
and the result of outside influences. Job, in his adversity,
knew both turmoil within and a sense of judgment from
without: 'If I am guilty – woe to me! Even if I am innocent, I
cannot lift my head, for I am full of shame and drowned in my
affliction' (Job 10:15). These feelings of shame and God's
disapproval were heightened by the incessant opposition of
his lecturing, hectoring 'friends'; he complains that these
younger men mock him in song and says of them, 'I have
become a byword among them. They detest me and keep

their distance; they do not hesitate to spit in my face' (Job 30:9,10).

Few, if any of us, have to cope with that degree of hostility in our afflictions. Or do we? Are there not, at least for some, elements of mockery, a keeping of a distance and, in a metaphorical sense, a spitting in the face. Sometimes these come about because people give up on us. We have been ill or incapacitated for far too long. Such can tire of visiting, phoning, writing letters, helping with practicalities. We sense their turning away, their disapproval even. We do not know whether they now think of us and, if they do, we can only guess their thoughts might be: 'Isn't it about time he snapped out of it?' 'I think she rather enjoys being out of action'; 'I always felt he was inadequate, a non-coper; now I know it!' Observations like these may, of course, have more than a grain of truth in them, but they tend to be the observations of those who have stepped back from everyday contact with those they comment on.

At other times, the rejection by those who look on relates to the nature of our infirmity. There have always been conditions which, for a variety of reasons, have led to abhorrence and distancing: leprosy, the plague, tuberculosis, venereal diseases, and so on. In certain cultures the list has been a longer one, sometimes because of the equation made between certain medical states and specific sins. Judaism, for instance, in the intertestamental period, lapsed into this attitude, declaring, 'Ulcers and dropsy are on account of immorality and licentiousness, quinsy on account of neglecting tithes, leprosy on account of blasphemy, blood-shed and perjury, epilepsy and the crippling of children on account of marital infidelity.'[8]

Perhaps, today, it is the condition of AIDS (Acquired Immune Deficiency Syndrome) which is arousing the greatest reaction amongst the morally indignant. Such see this tragic, new and fatal disease as the judgment of God on a sexually profligate world. Although there is no doubt that the prime vehicle of the spread of the AIDS virus has been the genital activities of homosexual and bisexual men, compounded by the worlds of intravenous drug abuse and prostitution, there is now an increasing danger of wide transmission amongst heterosexual contacts. Thus, together with those such as haemophiliacs infected through receiving blood products, it is increasingly likely that many whose lifestyle is one of sexual continence or marital faithfulness will fall to the 'stigma' of this affliction. Margaret Brearley, writing in *Third Way*, warns the Church that this 'unprecedented problem' will come very near home:

> There will be hundreds, perhaps thousands of Christian believers who will become the utterly innocent victims of AIDS (the spouses and babies of sufferers, as well as haemophiliacs and recipients of blood). How will they maintain their Christian faith intact? How will they learn to forgive? How will they learn not to despair, but to trust to God's mercy and grace throughout the course of their disease?[9]

AIDS, then, is perhaps the extreme example of the 'shame' an illness can incur. We do not need to be personally responsible for our sicknesses to feel the pain of conditions from which others turn away. In our sense of rejection and desertion let us take courage from the one who was made 'a curse for us' and who, having wrought our salvation through suffering, is 'not ashamed' to call us brothers and sisters.

As we have thought about the weakness and shame experienced by Christ we have seen, too, how, in his identification with our human frailty, he takes on our mortality. He accepts the requirements and limitations of a physical body: the need for work, rest, sleep, warmth, food and drink; the finiteness of being tied to only one place at one moment, of having limited strength and of coping with all the restrictions of space and time. As we know, he was unprotected not only from tiredness, hunger and thirst but also from pain, incapacity, dying and death itself. He is the Lamb of God who 'poured out his life unto death' (Isa 53:12).

When Jesus says, 'If anyone would come after me, he must deny himself and take up his cross and follow me' (Mt 16:24) we see the challenge to take the direction of 'No' to selfish interest and 'Yes' to God's way – the way of weakness and shame, vulnerability and ridicule that keeps in step with the Christ. This route is often portrayed as one of close friendship with the Lord in his dying and death. It seems that any suffering we go through in his name is part of, and even an extension of, his sufferings. Paul writes: 'We always carry around in our body the death of Jesus, so that the life of Jesus may also be revealed in our body' (2 Co 4:10); and, similarly: 'I fill up in my flesh what is still lacking in regard to Christ's afflictions, for the sake of his body, which is the church' (Col 1:24); and, further, makes it part of his prayer that he may know Christ 'and the fellowship of sharing in his sufferings, becoming like him in his death' (Php 3:10).

Those who know the adversity of persistent or serious illness are often drawn very near to the Christ who suffers. Robert Foxcroft, formerly an army chaplain, and, later, vicar of St Peter's, Hammersmith and a well known broadcaster with the BBC, died on New Year's Day, 1986 at the age of forty-five, after battling with cancer for nearly three years.[10] He was a man who could communicate about his suffering with a great variety of rich imagery. He compared coping with cancer to rock-climbing, in that 'it's all right as long as you don't look down.' He also picked up the analogy of life as a journey, through a snatch of conversation with his young daughter. He asked her, 'What are you doing in the school Nativity Play?' and she replied, 'I'm nothing; I'm just a traveller.' It was the idea of travelling, along with the call to follow Christ's path of suffering, that led to his widely acclaimed radio talks in Holy Week, the year before he died. Using the concept of a railway journey, they were entitled, 'All Stations to the Cross.'

Theme of Healing

Throughout our consideration of the weakness, shame and overall mortality of our earthly existence there has been a sense of something more waiting in the wings. We have, so far in this final chapter, majored on the theme of suffering but, as we have argued before, we live in 'in-between' times, and the power and glory of eternity threaten to burst in on to the stage of life. In fact, since the coming of Christ the new age has been ushered in. The Lord himself declared its inauguration in these messianic words from Isaiah:

> The Spirit of the Lord is on me, because he has anointed me to preach good news to the poor. He has sent me to proclaim freedom for the prisoners and recovery of sight for the blind, to release the oppressed, to proclaim the year of the Lord's favour (Lk 4:18,19).

In spite of the vast repository of humanity's continuing afflictions, here there is confident proclamation of an about-turn in the destiny of countless men, women and children. Every victory over sin, sickness, deformity, incapacity and all forms of oppression is a foretaste of the kingdom's full and final triumph.

At the climax of that triumph we, like Christ before us, shall rise again. Our present earthly bodies, unless the Lord returns first, will, like the seed that is sown, disintegrate in death and so, like the shoot, plant and fruit which grow from the seed, will be raised up: there will be both continuity and transformation. As we have already quoted, 'The body that is sown is perishable, it is raised imperishable; it is sown in dishonour, it is raised in glory, it is sown in weakness, it is raised in power.'[11]

We have considered the weakness and shame of our everyday lives as we follow Christ; let us now reflect on the power and glory which are the hallmarks of his kingdom – both, in part, in the 'here and now' and, in their entirety, in eternity.

1. Power

In Revelation 4 and 5, John sets the first of many scenes in which he describes, as best he can, both the wonders and terrors of the 'last things'. Here his vision is centred on 'a throne in heaven with someone sitting on it' (Rev 4:2). We realise that this someone is none other than God himself as the 'four living creatures' declare, day and night: 'Holy, holy, holy is the Lord God Almighty who was, and is, and is to come' (Rev 4:8). As the focus of the scene changes, John sees in God's right hand a sealed scroll which no one seems worthy to open. No one, that is, till one of the elders speaks to the grieving apostle, 'Do not weep! See, the Lion of the tribe of Judah, the Root of David, has triumphed. He is able to open the scroll and its seven seals' (Rev 5:5).

Here is a clear reference to Christ, of the house of David, who had been foretold by Jacob in these somewhat cryptic words; 'You are a lion's club, O Judah... Like a lion he crouches and lies down, like a lioness – who dares to rouse him? The sceptre will not depart from Judah... until he comes to whom it belongs and the obedience of the nations is his' (Ge 49:9,10). Without attempting a detailed interpretation of Jacob's prophecy or John's vision, we have here a picture of Christ which is a far cry from the symbolism of the Lamb, who is weak, vulnerable, submissive and sacrificial. Now we see the Lord as like the Lion: strong, bold, triumphant, kingly, executing judgment.

As the revelations to John continue, we reach one of those unexpected transformations that can be the stuff of dreams. For as he looks at the Lion of Judah, strong and imperious, he sees a lamb! 'Then I saw a Lamb, looking as if it had been slain, standing in the centre of the throne...' (Rev 5:6). We return now to the imagery of Jesus as 'the Lamb of God, who takes away the sin of the world' (John 1:29) – and yet we have moved on, for the picture is not now one of shame, weakness and defeat, but of power and glory. Indeed, 'ten thousand times ten thousand' angels are heard singing praises to him: 'Worthy is the Lamb, who was slain, to receive power and wealth and wisdom and strength and honour and glory and praise!' (Rev 5:12). Furthermore, as the tone of John's vision changes with the opening of the seals, we are shown not only a powerful and glorious Lamb, but a wrathful Lamb who brings judgment on those who oppose God (Rev 6:15-17).

Although a glimpse of the 'last things' and eternity reveals a portrayal of Christ as a wrathful Lamb and a strong Lion, we see, too, throughout his earthly life many manifestations of heavenly power. We should stand back in wonder at the Christ who proclaims 'the year of the Lord's favour' and thus ushers in the new age, overpowering the Enemy and all his works in a thousand and one ways. The blind see, the deaf hear, the sick are healed, the paralysed can walk again, the sinful are forgiven, the world-weary find peace, the demon-possessed are released and the dead are raised up. Beyond such immediate victories, the Lord brings his revolutionary teaching, which declares a way of life that is lived in obedience to the Father, in companionship with the Son and in the strength of the Spirit. The ground-rules for the kingdom of God are laid out for personal and communal response, which will, in turn, challenge and advance on the forces of darkness throughout the centuries of the 'in-between' times. Satan, the 'strong man', is 'bound' and 'robbed' by one who is even stronger, the man Christ Jesus (Mk 3:23-27). Peter, at Pentecost, addresses the crowd and announces that the Spirit's outpouring marks the 'last days', which have also been heralded by the all-powerful Son of God; he says:

> Men of Israel, listen to this: Jesus of Nazareth was a man accredited by God to you by miracles, wonders and signs, which God did among you through him, as you yourselves know (Ac 2:22).

This accreditation by God is given its final seal in the triumph of the Lord over the bondage of death itself. Peter continues, 'God raised him from the dead, freeing him from the agony of death, because it was impossible for death to keep his hold on him' (Ac 2:24).

The resurrection of Jesus is extremely good news for us all. For just as his dying is the gateway to our release from the guilt of the past, so his rising again is the guarantee of power to live the new life – a life marked by both the way of the cross and the way of the empty tomb. Paul, in 2 Corinthians 13:4, declares the double perspective of dying and living, of weakness and strength, which is the essence of our calling to serve God and one another:

> For to be sure, he was crucified in weakness, yet he lives by God's power. Likewise, we are weak in him, yet by God's power we will live with him to serve you.

Notice that the emphasis in this verse is living by *God's* power. Human nature, by itself, is not very good with power. Lord Acton's famous dictum, taken from a letter written in 1887 to a bishop friend, is still worth repeating: 'Power tends to corrupt and absolute power corrupts absolutely.' There is an opposing truth attributed to Adlai Stevenson in the early 1960s: 'Power corrupts, but lack of power corrupts absolutely.' We can say from these two maxims that we need some degree of power to function but that too much power is not good for us. The Bible clearly puts the stress on our weakness and vulnerability, and yet also on the availability of God's power in the continuing struggle against Enemy forces. We are called to 'be strong in the Lord and in his mighty power' (Eph 6:10); each of us can declare, 'I can do everything through him who gives me strength' (Php 4:13); and, as an overarching perspective for our daily lives, we read that Christ himself is 'the power of God' (1 Co 1:24).

There is no doubt that, since the 1960s, the Holy Spirit has been reminding the Church once more that God is a God of 'mighty works': the so-called 'charismatic', 'renewal' and 'restoration' movements, together with the work of John Wimber of the Vineyard Christian Fellowship, have majored on the power of God in church growth, evangelism and healing. And yet, because the finiteness of our humanity tends to respond to a neglected truth with overemphasis, in many quarters there has been a tendency to so stress 'signs and wonders' that the evidences for God's work become more important than him to whom they should point, and what should be seen as a foretaste of glory to come is treated as a main course for the here and now.[12]

Even so, for those who are ill, as we saw in chapter three, there is a natural desire for some manifestation of the Lord's power to intervene. We saw then that God is sovereign, that he may choose healing, immediate or gradual, through a variety of means or he may offer his daily strength amidst continuing affliction; we observed too that God is Father and delights to give us good gifts, in his own time and way. Whatever his will for the details of our lives, we can observe his power at work; may be through healing, partial or complete, spontaneous or delayed; may be through a strengthening to overcome frustration and limitation; may be through reconciliation between an awkward patient and a despairing carer; may be through a deep sense of peace in the face of death.

It has been said that 'next to power without honour, the most dangerous thing in the world is power without humour,' and sometimes God's enabling shines clearest where there is laughter. One friend, whose wife was dying of cancer, was inundated by numerous gifts of flowers. Every special delivery brought more choice blooms to fill the rooms. As I emerged one day from this veritable Kew Gardens, he turned to me with a twinkle in his eye and said, 'If you or Joy get seriously ill, the first thing to do is to buy twelve vases!' I thought this was an underestimate when I heard too of the large number of sprays soaking in various buckets of water about the house.

The power that sustains us, day by day, as we confront sickness and dying, is the power that will also one day raise us up. In the meantime, unless the Lord comes first, we all have to face death itself. As Woody Allen puts it, 'Death is an acquired trait' and, we might add, this is the one acquired trait that we have no option over! Jonathan, as we have seen, though fearful of dying, was not afraid of death and its inevitability. Nor need he have been, for although 'The sting of death is sin, and the power of sin is the law' (1 Co 15:56), he had, in Christ, been freed from the shackles of guilt and the condemnation which the requirements of God's law bring. We too can anticipate Christ's triumph both in removing the venom which death holds for many and in his promise that, at his coming, death, 'the last enemy' (1 Co 15:26) will be finally destroyed. The 'acquired trait' will be no more.

2. Glory

Glory is one of the great words of the Bible. The Greek *doxa* simply meant 'option for conjecture' in the secular world, but its biblical use came to signify 'glory, repute, radiance'. Although used to honour angels, human beings and the wonders of the created order, *doxa* speaks supremely of the glory of God, of his glorious revealing of himself.[13] During the wanderings of the Israelites God's radiant glory was localised, as it were, in the tabernacle, (Ex 40:34-38); in Isaiah's vision, although the train of the robe of 'the King, the Lord Almighty' filled the temple, the seraphs sang, 'the whole earth is full of his glory' (Isa 6:1-5); later, Isaiah prophesied that the Lord God's glory would appear over his people and that, with the winding up of history, 'the Lord will be your everlasting light, and your God will be your glory' (Isa 60:19).

As we have already said, it is Jesus who comes to inaugurate the new age, the age of the 'in-between' times when God's power and glory break through into the weakness and shame of our earthly existence. As John writes:

> The Word became flesh and made his dwelling among us.
> We have seen his glory, the glory of the One and Only,
> who came from the Father, full of grace and truth (Jn
> 1:14).

This 'glory of the One and Only', though manifest in every word and action of his life, was glimpsed in its eternal intensity by Peter and the Zebedee brothers when he 'led them up a high mountain by themselves'. His radiant splendour is described in these words: 'There he was transfigured before them. His face shone like the sun and his clothes became as white as the light' (Mt 17:2). Even though his full glory was revealed to his dazzled and dazed followers on this occasion, we should see that both glory and shame were inextricably bound up together as he faced death. In his great prayer to the Father in the upper room, Jesus is aware that the ignominy of his very dying is also the path of glory:

> Father, the time has come. Glorify your Son, that your Son may glorify you... And now, Father, glorify me in your presence with the glory I had with you before the world began (Jn 17:1,5).

And just as we have realised that we are to partake of his weakness, shame and power, we are also recipients of his glory. Here, once again, the way of the cross and the empty tomb are interwoven. Jesus declares, on the eve of his crucifixion, that he had passed on the glory he had received from his Father to his disciples (Jn 17:22); later, after his resurrection, he speaks of Peter's coming death and John writes, 'Jesus said this to indicate the kind of death by which Peter *would glorify God*' (Jn 21:19, italics mine).

More generally, in the same way that our Lord's path of suffering was not only a path where glory broke through but a path into eternal glory, so it is for us. It is as we share in Christ's adversities that we have both foretastes of glory and the sure promise of glory's fruition. In Colossians 1:27, we see how God makes known to his people 'the riches' of his glory now and, further, how Christ in the life of the believer is 'the hope of glory'. Romans 8:17-25 not only establishes the link between sharing in Christ's sufferings 'in order that we may also share in his glory' (verse 17) but also demonstrates that the twin theme of affliction and glorification is on a cosmic scale: for 'the creation itself will be liberated from its bondage to decay and brought into the glorious freedom of the children of God' (verse 21) The Bible promises not only a new heaven but a new earth; and when we contemplate, on the one hand, the pain, cruelty and disintegration and, on the other hand, the beauty, unity and complexity of the created world, we can surely rejoice that a 'glorious freedom' is promised for the old order.

Sharing in Christ's glory can also be expressed in terms of our becoming more like him. Glory is infectious! Just as Moses, quite unwittingly, 'was radiant because he had spoken with the Lord' (Ex 34:29) so we, through our daily encounters with Christ, begin to 'catch' something of his glory:

> And we, who with unveiled faces all reflect [or, contemplate] the Lord's glory, are being transformed into his likeness with ever-increasing glory, which comes from the Lord, who is the Spirit (2 Co 3:18).

Unlike Moses, whose radiance was fleeting, our own transformation, through the Spirit's work, is a process of 'ever-increasing glory'. Indeed, this enterprise of change will reach its climax when Christ comes again: 'when he appears we shall be like him, for we shall see him as he is' (1 Jn 3:2). As he returns he 'will transform our lowly bodies so that they will be like his glorious body' (Php 3:21). Once again, we are with the mystery and wonderment of our bodily resurrection. Sons and daughters of 'the first man Adam', creatures of weakness, shame and mortality, we are to be raised up, bearing the likeness of Jesus Christ, 'the last Adam' – immortal, strong and glorious (1 Co 15:42-49). C. S. Lewis captures something of the wonder of it all on the closing page of *The Last Battle*:

> 'There *was* a real railway accident,' said Aslan softly. 'Your father and mother and all of you are – as you used to call it in the Shadowlands – dead. The term is over: the holidays have begun. The dream is ended: this is the morning.'[14]

What does all this talk of resurrection and glory have to say to you and me in the daily turmoil which illness and dying can bring upon us? In the midst of our weakness, vulnerability and shame, our lives can seem far removed from Christ's final victory over death and the sound of countless numbers praising the glorified Lamb of God. Our everyday existence seems caught up more with the misunderstandings and insensitivities of trying to cope with the immediate. Sometimes a passing remark cuts deeply, as when one earnest enquirer asked a young woman in her mid-twenties, following an X-ray report which queried cancer, 'Is it terminal?' At other times there may be an element of private humour which can just about alleviate the pain. On one occasion, soon after my eighteen months or so in and out of blindness, and while I was still feeling raw about the whole experience, I was part of the following interchange. I was asked by someone I hardly knew, 'How about your seeing people these days?' Assuming this was a concerned question about my eyesight, I replied, 'Really – very good!' My interrogator continued, 'Oh, good! Then I'll tell Jean, and perhaps she'll come to see you for counselling'!

At a profounder level, C. S. Lewis, wrestling with the harrowing experience of bereavement, sought to come to terms with the stark reality of his loneliness in these words:

> Imagine a man in total darkness. He thinks he is in a cellar or dungeon. Then there comes a sound. He thinks it might be a sound from far off – waves or wind-blown trees or cattle half a mile away. And if so, it proves he's not in a cellar, but free, in the open air. Or it may be a much smaller sound close at hand – a chuckle of laughter. And if so, there is a friend just beside him in the dark. Either way, a good, good sound. I'm not mad enough to take such an experience as evidence for anything. It is simply the leaping into imaginative activity of an idea which I would always have theoretically admitted – the idea that I, or any mortal at any time, may be utterly mistaken as to the situation he is really in.[15]

Later, and more specifically, he is able to write that, in heaven, 'we shall see that there never was any problem' and of the bodily resurrection, 'We cannot understand. The best is perhaps what we understand least.'[16]

Many of us live lives which, for long stretches, feel like those of someone 'in total darkness': we are, perhaps, trying to endure a painful illness, the frustrations of disability or the aching void of losing a person who meant so much to us. Then 'there comes a sound', one of C. S. Lewis's 'good good sounds', like the chuckle of a friend close by, and we realise that, in some way, we have been mistaken. We are not in 'a cellar or dungeon' but 'in the open air'. Maybe this breath of some other, fresher perspective comes to us through the smile of a loved one, a snatch of bird song, the sun on our faces, a piece of familiar music or perhaps, less tangibly though no less certainly, through some inner conviction, some new appreciation of one of our Lord's sayings, some sense of joy or peace, a feeling that, after all, all will be well. At moments like these we realise something of the wonder and, yet, straightforwardness of it all. Lewis describes this as the 'sense that some shattering and disarming simplicity is the real answer.'[17]

On the tombstone of Lord Baden-Powell, the founder of the Scouting movement, the few words inscribed are accompanied by a circle with a dot at its centre. This is a woodcraft symbol for 'gone home', and it is that sense of 'going home' to be with the Lord and his departed people which seems to me to be the essence of C.S. Lewis's 'shattering and disarming simplicity'. I have the feeling of an unsurpassed level of domestic welcome as I recall my own father's terminal illness a few years ago. At one point, while dying of cancer and yet before the stroke which incapacitated his last weeks, he dreamt a vivid dream that signified, perhaps, his somewhat mixed memories of his own earlier family life. He was, in fact, the last survivor of his generation of Hurdings, and, in his dream, the end of his bed was crowded by his deceased parents, brothers and sisters, who appeared to wait eagerly for him to join them. At that stage he was not prepared to cross the 'great divide' for, within the dream, he cried out at his erstwhile relatives, 'Go away! I'm not ready to join you lot yet!'

Even so, during his remaining weeks, there was no question

of his increasing preparedness for his own homecoming. His faith in Christ was simple, without being simplistic, and, at a certain stage in his decline, though speechless due to his stroke, he clearly resinged himself to his coming death. Whether to be welcomed by family or not, he was ready to meet his Lord. Although our fondness for him may have coloured our imagination, my mother, sister and I, witnessing his last few moments and observing the backward sweep of his grey hair on the pillow and the peacefulness of his worn and wasted face, had a sense of his frail and windswept body arrowing through the clouds to a tumultuous welcome. Home at last!

For those of us who remain, we cannot deny that our lives are often a struggle and that the sound of a 'chuckle in the darkness' seems hardly ever to be our experience. Let us take the encouragement which the way of the cross and the way of the empty tomb offer us; suffering may be our theme now but wholeness shall be our theme then. As Paul writes:

> Therefore we do not lose heart. Though outwardly we are wasting away, yet inwardly we are being renewed day by day. For our light and momentary troubles are achieving for us an eternal glory that far outweighs them all (2 Co 4:16,17).

James Casson, a general practitioner dying at the age of thirty-seven and leaving a wife and two children, knew the way of weakness and power, shame and glory. Like many of us he had cried out for healing. In reality, as his body wasted away he also had glimpses, amidst the pain and anger, of a daily renewing which would bring him to perfect wholeness. At the conclusion of his book *Dying: the greatest adventure of my life*, he wrote this of his final journey home:

> One morning I had a clear picture that I was in a boat. Before, when asking for healing, it was as though I was in a punt where one stands at one end pushing on the punt pole and steering with more or less expertise. Afterwards, I was in a rowing boat, my back to the direction I was

going, but travelling in a much more leisurely fashion. The great joy was that the Lord was at the tiller, his face gently smiling and his eyes twinkling as he quietly guided me to my destination.

Was I healed? Yes I believe I was.[18]

NOTES

Chapter One

1. For a fuller account of the story, see Roger F. Hurding, *As Trees Walking* (Exeter: The Paternoster Press 1982).
2. W. Somerset Maugham, *The Moon and Sixpence* (Pan 1974) p. 64.
3. For more on Paul Tournier's life and thinking, see Gary R. Collins (ed.) *Helping People Grow* (Santa Ana: Vision House 1980) pp. 55ff. and Roger F. Hurding, *Roots & Shoots: a guide to counselling and psychotherapy* (London: Hodder & Stoughton 1986) pp. 317ff.
4. Henri J. M. Nouwen, *Reaching Out* (Glasgow: Collins/Fount Paperbacks 1980) p. 42.

Chapter Two

1. Colin Brown (ed.) *The New International Dictionary of New Testament Theology* (Exeter: The Paternoster Press 1975) Vol. 1 p. 109; see pp. 105–13 for a useful section on 'anger' in the New Testament.
2. Duncan Buchanan, *The Counselling of Jesus* (London: Hodder & Stoughton 1985) p. 57.
3. John White, *The Masks of Melancholy* (Leicester: IVP 1982); see especially, pp. 75–100.
4. For a fuller section on mood change in men, see John Nicholson, *Men & Women: how different are they?* (Oxford: Oxford University Press 1984) pp. 66–9.
5. For helpful accounts of physical aspects of understanding and treating depression, see John White, *op. cit.*, pp. 205–

222 and Richard Winter, *The Roots of Sorrow* (Basingstoke: Marshall, Morgan & Scott 1985) pp. 49–63.
6. Colin Brown, *DNTT* Vol. 2, p. 420.
7. John Job, *Where is My Father?: studies in the Book of Job* (London: Epworth Press 1977) p. 31.
8. C. S. Lewis, *The Problem of Pain* (Glasgow: Collins/Fontana Paperbacks 1977) p. 74.

Chapter Three

1. Henry W. Frost *Miraculous Healing: a personal testimony and biblical study* (London: Oliphants 1957) pp. 114–15.
2. Morton Kelsey, *Healing and Christianity* (London: SCM Press 1973) Chapter 4.
3. For a fuller consideration of our Lord's healing ministry see Roger F. Hurding 'Healing' in Bernard Palmer (ed.), *Medicine and the Bible* (Exeter: The Paternoster Press 1986) pp. 196–203.
4. See, for example, Wilhelm Mundle in Colin Brown (ed.), *Dictionary of New Testament Theology* Vol. 2 pp. 620–1.
5. Henry W. Frost, *op. cit.,* p. 87.
6. Quoted in David Clines 'A Biblical Doctrine of Man', *The Journal of the Christian Brethren Research Fellowship* 28 (1976) p. 10.
7. Morris Maddocks, *The Christian Healing Ministry* (London: SPCK 1981) p. 10.
8. Paul Tournier, *Creative Suffering* (SCM 1982) p. 44.
9. See Gerard W. Hughes, *God of Surprises* (London: Darton, Longman & Todd 1985).
10. J. I. Packer, *Knowing God* (London: Hodder & Stoughton 1975) p. 97.
11. C.F.D. Moule in Thomas A. Smail, *The Forgotten Father* (Hodder & Stoughton 1980) p. 39; see pp. 38–39 for this section on *Abba*.
12. Kathryn Kuhlmann, *I Believe in Miracles* (Oliphants 1963) p. 10.

13. Francis MacNutt, *Healing* (New York: Bantam Books 1977) p. 102.
14. Colin Brown, *DNTT* Vol. 1, p. 727.
15. John Wimber and Kevin Springer, *Power Healing* (Hodder & Stoughton 1986) p. 169.

Chapter Four

1. George Orwell, *Animal Farm* (Harmondsworth: Penguin 1951 pp. 97–8.
2. From Ellen Wilkie, *Pithy Poems* (London: Imp Press 1985), obtainable from the author at 54 Whitby Court, Parkhurst Road, London N7 0SU. Used with permission.
3. For the law of Christ that is the law of love and gives freedom, see Galatians 5:13, 14; 6:2; and James 1:25; 2:12.
4. See Elaine Brook and Julie Donnelly, *The Windhorse* (London: Jonathan Cape 1986).
5. For the hallmarks of friendship in the Book of Proverbs, see Derek Kidner, *Proverbs: an introduction and commentary* (London: IVP 1964) p. 45.
6. C. S. Lewis, *The Four Loves* (London: Collins 1963) p. 91.
7. Carlo Carretto, *Why O Lord? the inner meaning of suffering* (London: Darton, Longman & Todd 1986) p. 45.
8. See Henri J. M. Nouwen, *The Wounded Healer* (New York: Doubleday & Co. 1979) pp. 81–2.
9. *Shorter Oxford English Dictionary*.
10. Richard Holloway, *The Killing: meditations on the death of Christ* (London: Darton, Longman & Todd 1984) p. 57.

Chapter Five

1. Alastair V. Campbell, *Paid to Care? the limits of professionalism in pastoral care* (London: SPCK 1985) p. 50.

2. Alexander Solzhenitsyn, *Cancer Ward* (Penguin 1971) p. 278.
3. Attributed to La Rochefoucauld (1613–1680).
4. Elisabeth Kübler-Ross *On Death and Dying* (London: Tavistock Publications 1970) p. 48.
5. *ibid.*, p. 100.
6. The word 'hospice' has a long history and originally implied 'both host and guest'; it signifies giving and receiving. In the Middle Ages, hospices were places of refreshment for travellers. The modern Hospice Movement has its origins in the work of Dame Cicely Saunders, who founded St Christopher's Hospice, Sydenham in 1967. Today there are four main models: the separate, bedded hospice; the Continuing Care Unit, based on a hospital campus and sharing facilities with the hospital; the Home Care Team; and the Hospital Support Team, a consulting service which seeks to integrate principles of terminal care with General Practice. See Shirley du Boulay *Cicely Saunders* (Hodder & Stoughton 1984) pp. 226–31.
7. See Donald Capps, *Biblical Approaches in Pastoral Counseling* (Philadelphia: The Westminster Press 1981) p. 52.
8. *ibid.*, p. 76.
9. *ibid.*, pp. 84–85.
10. *Guardian* 22 April 1986.
11. Claus Westermann, quoted by Capps, p. 72.
12. Donald Capps, *op. cit.*, p. 87.

Chapter Six

1. Julian of Norwich, *Revelations of Divine Love,* transl. Clifton Wolters (Penguin 1966) p. 74.
2. Colin Brown (ed.), *Dictionary of New Testament Theology* Vol. 3 p. 993.
3. Richard J. Foster *Celebration of Discipline: the path to spiritual growth* (Hodder & Stoughton 1980) p. 101.

4. Paul Tournier, *The Strong and the Weak* (SCM Press 1963) pp. 20–21.
5. See Deuteronomy 21: 22, 23; Galatians 3: 13, 14.
6. Dick Keyes, *Beyond Identity: finding yourself in the image and character of God* (Hodder & Stoughton 1986) p. 52.
7. *ibid.,* p. 92.
8. Kittel (ed.), *Theological Dictionary of the New Testament* Vol. 3 (Grand Rapids: Eerdmans 1965) p. 201.
9. Margaret Brearley, 'Scarred yet Singing: Jack Clemo – life and work' *Third Way* (Oct. 1986) Vol. 9 No. 10 p. 24.
10. Details from John Barton, 'In Memoriam: Robert Gill Bentley Foxcroft' *Church of England Newspaper* Jan. 10, 1986 and tribute on *Sunday*, Radio Four, Jan. 1986.
11. See 1 Corinthians 15: 35–58.
12. For sympathetic critiques of the 'Charismatic renewal' movement, see Richard F. Lovelace, *Dynamics of Spiritual Life* (The Paternoster Press 1979) pp. 261–70 and Thomas A. Smail *The Forgotten Father* (Hodder & Stoughton 1980) pp. 13–20.
13. See Colin Brown (ed.), *DNTT* Vol. 2 pp. 44–8.
14. C. S. Lewis, *The Last Battle* (Penguin 1964) p. 165.
15. C. S. Lewis, *A Grief Observed* (Faber & Faber 1961) pp. 50–1.
16. *ibid.,* pp. 56, 59.
17. *ibid.,* p. 56.
18. James H. Casson, *Dying: the greatest adventure of my life* (London: Christian Medical Fellowship 1980) p. 37.

SUGGESTED READING

Coping with illness

Mary Moster, *Living With Cancer* (Hodder & Stoughton 1988).

Roger F. Hurding, *As Trees Walking* (The Paternoster Press 1982). On coping with diabetes and blindness.

John Job, *Where is My Father? Studies in the Book of Job* (Epworth Press 1977).

C. S. Lewis, *The Problem of Pain* (Collins/Fontana 1986).

Edith Schaeffer, *Affliction* (Hodder & Stoughton 1984).

Basilea Schlink, *The Blessings of Illness* (Marshalls 1984).

Paul Tournier, *Creative Suffering* (SCM Press 1982).

Coping with disability

Carlo Carretto, *Why O Lord? The Inner Meaning of Suffering* (Darton, Longman & Todd 1986).

Mary Craig, *Blessings* (Hodder & Stoughton 1979). On coping with handicapped children.

Joni Eareckson, *Joni* (Pickering & Inglis 1978).

Pennie Kidd, *I'm Smiling as Hard as I Can* (Mowbray 1981). On coping with multiple sclerosis.

Jennifer Rees Larcombe, *Beyond Healing* (Hodder & Stoughton 1986).

Max Sinclair, *Halfway to Heaven* (Hodder & Stoughton 1982). Like *Joni,* on coping with physical paralysis.

Jean Vanier, *Man and Woman He Made Them* (Darton, Longman & Todd 1985). On relationships and sexuality amongst the handicapped.

Healing

Ann England, (ed.), *We Believe in Healing* (Marshalls 1982).

Rex Gardner, *Healing Miracles* (Darton, Longman & Todd 1986).

Henry W. Frost, *Miraculous Healing* (Marshall, Morgan & Scott 1961).

Roger F. Hurding, 'Healing' in Bernard Palmer (ed.), *Medicine and the Bible* (The Paternoster Press 1986).

C. S. Lewis *Miracles* (Collins/Fontana 1960).

Francis MacNutt, *Healing* (Bantam 1977).

Francis MacNutt, *The Power to Heal* (Ave Maria Press 1977).

Morris Maddocks, *The Christian Healing Ministry* (SPCK 1981).

Derek Williams, *Not Once, But Twice: The Tim Dean Story* (Hodder & Stoughton 1987).

John Wimber with Kevin Springer, *Power Healing* (Hodder & Stoughton 1986).

Living with dying

James H. Casson, *Dying: The Greatest Adventure of My Life* (Christian Medical Fellowship 1980).

John Hinton, *Dying* (Penguin 1972).

Ruth L. Kopp with Stephen Sorenson, *Encounter with Terminal Illness* (Lion Publishing 1981).

Elisabeth Kübler-Ross, *On Death and Dying* (Tavistock Publications 1973).

Peter L. Sampson, *The Courage to Hope* (Scripture Union 1987)

David Watson, *Fear No Evil* (Hodder & Stoughton 1984).

Living with death

Elizabeth Collick, *Through Grief: The Bereavement Journey* (Darton, Longman & Todd 1986).

Jim Graham, *Dying to Live: The Christian Teaching on Life after Death* (Marshalls 1984).

Marjorie Holmes, *To Help You Through the Hurting* (Hodder & Stoughton 1983).

C. S. Lewis, *A Grief Observed* (Faber & Faber 1966).

Colin Murray Parkes, *Bereavement: Studies of Grief in Adult Life* (Penguin 1986).

Jean Richardson, *A Death in the Family* (Lion Publishing 1982). A practical guide, illustrated.

SOME USEFUL ADDRESSES

General

The Terence Higgins Trust, BM AIDS, London, WC1N 3XX (01-278 8745).

Arthritis Care, 6 Grosvenor Crescent, London, SW1X 7ER (01-235 0902).

Back Pain Association, Grundy House, 31–33 Park Road, Teddington, TW11 0AB (01-977 5474/5).

The Chest, Heart and Stroke Association, Tavistock House North, Tavistock Square, London, WC1H 9JE (01-387 3012).

The Coeliac Society for the United Kingdom, PO Box No. 181, London, NW2 2QY (01-459 2440).

Colostomy Welfare Group, 38/39 Eccleston Square, London, SW1V 1PB (01-828 5175).

Cystic Fibrosis Research Trust, Alexandra House, 5 Blyth Road, Bromley, Kent, BR1 3RS (01-464 7211).

British Diabetic Association, 10 Queen Anne Street, London, W1M 0BD (01-323 1531).

The British Digestive Foundation, 7 Chandos Street, Cavendish Square, London, W1A 2LN (01-580 1155).

The National Eczema Society, Tavistock House North, Tavistock Square, London, WC1H 9SR (01-388 4097).

The British Epilepsy Association, Anstey House, 40 Hanover Square, Leeds, L53 1BE (0532 439393).

The Epilepsy Association of Scotland, 48 Govan Road, Glasgow, G51 1JJ (041-427 4911).

Haemophilia Society, 123 Westminster Bridge Road, London, SE1 7HR (01-928 2020).

Ileostomy Association of Great Britain and Ireland, Amblehurst House, Chobham, Woking, Surrey, GU24 8PZ.

The Myalgic Encephalomeyelitis Association, The Moss, Third Avenue, Standford-le-Hope, Essex, SS17 8EL (0375 642466). Offers help for those suffering from 'post-viral syndrome'.

National Federation of Kidney Patients' Associations, Acorn Lodge, Woodsetts, nr. Worksop, Notts., S81 8AT (0909 562703).

Parkinson's Disease Society of the United Kingdom, 36 Portland Place, London, W1N 3DG (01-323 1174).

The Psoriasis Association, 7 Milton Street, Northampton, NN2 7JG (0604 711129).

Urostomy Association, 'Buckland', Beaumont Park, Danbury, Essex, CM3 4DE (024 541 4294).

Cancer Care

Hospice Information Service, St Christopher's Hospice, 51/59 Lawrie Park Road, Sydenham, London, SE26 6DZ (01-778 1240).

Marie Curie Memorial Foundation, 28 Belgrave Square, London, SW1X 8QG (01-235 3325). Provides help for many aspects of cancer problems.

The National Society for Cancer Relief, Anchor House, 15–19 Britten Street, London, SW3 3TY (01-351 7811). One aspect of their work is to provide Home Care Nursing through Macmillan nurses.

Hodgkin's Disease Association, PO Box 275, Haddenham, Aylesbury, Bucks. (0844 291 500).

Leukaemia Care Society, Box No. 82, Exeter, EX2 5DP (0392 218514).

Disability

The Royal National Institute for the Blind, 224 Great Portland Street, London, W1N 6AA (01-388 1266).

The Royal National Institute for the Deaf, 105 Gower Street, London, WC1E 6AH (01-387 8033).

Disabled Living Foundation, 380/384 Harrow Road, London, W9 2HU (01-289 6111). Concerned with non-medical aspects of daily lives of handicapped people and families.

Motor Neurone Disease Association, 61 Derngate, Northampton, NN1 1UE (0604 22269/250505).

The Multiple Sclerosis Society of Great Britain and Northern Ireland, 25 Effie Road, Fulham, London, SW6 1EE (01-736 6267).

Musclar Dystrophy Group of Great Britain and Northern Ireland, Nattrass House, 35 Macaulay Road, London, SW4 0QP (01-720 8055).

The British Polio Fellowship, Bell Close, West End Road, Ruislip, HA4 6LP (0895 675515).

The Spastics Society, 12 Park Crescent, London, W1N 4EQ (01-636 5020).

Association for Spina Bifida and Hydrocephalus, 22 Upper Woburn Place, London, WC1H 0EP (01-388 1382).

Spinal Injuries Association, Yeoman House, 76 St James's Lane, Muswell Hill, London, N10 3DF (01-444 2121).

FACING ANXIETY AND STRESS

Michael Lawson

'Remember those times when you have felt worried, irritable, tense and on edge, or even like running away? This book is written to help you understand and face anxiety and stress, and finally to overcome and rediscover peace and stability.'

Using lively illustrations of people encountering life's pressure points, Michael Lawson offers an accessible and encouraging self-help manual and a rich resource for those wanting to help others. 'The real, lasting power for effective change comes from God,' he affirms. 'The Spirit's presence in our lives means that change is possible.'

'Full of realism, reassurance and practical wisdom.' Richard Bewes, from his Foreword.

'Readable, realistic, reassuring and full of practical wisdom, a rich resource for these wanting to help others.'

CLC Floodtide

'It should be of great help to young Christians or to those on the fringes seeking a way forward, and will do much to help others recognise stress symptoms and face up to what is going on.'

Christian Weekly Newspapers

Michael Lawson is Director of Pastoring at All Souls, Langham Place in London.

ROOTS AND SHOOTS
A guide to counselling and psychotherapy

Roger F Hurding

Roots and Shoots traces the rise of secular psychologies and examines Christian responses to them. It studies a wide range of methods of counselling and psychotherapy, looking at assumptions, aims and techniques. It offers a framework for evaluating different styles and systems of counselling from a Christian perspective.

Roger Hurding argues that psychology and theology both have a part to play in a Christ-centred approach to counselling. His analysis and proposals will prove invaluable to Christian social workers, counsellors, psychotherapists and psychologists, psychiatrists, general practitioners and clergy. He is clear and compassionate, and his experience shines through to guide and inspire all those who wish to help and counsel others.

'The vision of the book is extensive and it has filled a real need in the British scene.'
British Journal of Medical Psychology

'A timely and important contribution to the debate surrounding counselling and pastoral care ... [it] demands and deserves to be widely read.'
Christian Arena

'A Christ-centred book which is also an objective and sensitive account of secular theories and therapies. Believers and non-believers will gain much from its useful syntheses and perspectives.'
Journal of the Royal College of General Practitioners

BEYOND HEALING

Jennifer Rees Larcombe

When Jennifer Rees Larcombe learned she had a rare viral disease that threatened her life, she was forced to rethink the issue of healing. Where do faith, sin and God's will come in and why, despite so much prayer, does she remain ill?

Jennifer's search for healing takes her to the outer reaches of faith and to the inner hurts and fears that might block God's power. Heartache and blessing go hand in hand, and Jennifer's relationship with God changes as she learns to suffer with him. Her stumbling progress towards an understanding of God's plans for her is recorded with disarming honesty, and her courage and humour will be an inspiration to all those who struggle in the face of suffering.

'Few will read it without being challenged and inspired.'
CLC Floodtide

'It is a spiritual education to read this book.'
The Officer

MAKING SENSE OUT OF SUFFERING

Peter Kreeft

Our world is full of billions of normal lives which have been touched by apparently pointless and random suffering. There can be few who have not struggled with this seemingly insurmountable obstacle to faith. This wise yet lively account succeeds in clarifying the issues, tackling the problems, and presenting the Christian answer. Glib, easy solutions are not provided: instead Peter Kreeft draws on philosophy, art, and biblical prophecy in seeking to understand suffering. Modernity cannot understand suffering, the author argues, and yet it is integral to our faith. This is not just a work of popular philosophy; it is a profound spiritual journey ending at the cross.

'Peter Kreeft takes up the unanswerable and carries us inexorably to the stunning answer.'

Elizabeth Elliot

Peter Kreeft is Professor of Philosophy at Boston College, U.S.A.